You Don't Need Social Media, Unless You Are Doing It Right.

The Small Business Guide to Social Media

Kristina Libby

For all my students.

May this save you the energy of buying me coffee.

Printed in the United States of America.

First Printing, 2016.

ISBN 0997715707

The Social Works Co
3017 Little Ml
The Colony, TX 75056

www.thesocialworksco.com

Table of Contents

What is Social Media?

Social media has been the buzz word of the past two decades and I have been in the thick of it. I've run my own social media agency, had successful personal profiles and grown social media channels for some of the biggest brands. Now, I teach a four semester practicum at the University of Florida, and have taught thousands of students in hundreds of classes globally about social media and how to effectively implement it for their businesses. Additionally, I've spent the past five years at Microsoft where I ran consumer PR for the brand. It's been a busy time, for the industry and for myself, and in that time social media has become the default answer for so many business marketing and sales conundrums.

All the noise about the power of social media has blurred the point: social media is a tool. Like all tools you must learn to yield it effectively but, there have been few books or programs to help you do so strategically.

Instead, information has been chucked at you. Billions of blogs and books and social media channels have talked about how to do social media but in almost all of the conversations, experts talk about social media for its own sake.

For the purposes of this book, think of social media not as a particular platform (like Twitter or Instagram) but as a strategic process that will contribute to the success of your business. The last part of that sentence is intentional – social media is about business. Social media success is about business success.

Let me interrupt to say something controversial: **You don't need social media.**

Social media is a tool. It's a tool that must align to your strategic business and goals. It's a tool that should help you to amplify and drive sales. If it is not doing those things, then you don't need social media.

You don't need to waste your time on something that is not providing you with business success. You don't need to waste time liking and posting and commenting and friending. You might as well not be doing anything on social media if you are going to go out there and do it without a coordinated and connected strategy. So, if you do want to do social media, if you do want to use it to increase your sales and to drive business impact, you need to figure out how to do it strategically using it as the tool it is.

How This Book Works

This book is an explanation of how to use a one-page tool that I devised after hundreds of hours of teaching entrepreneurs and small business owners about social media. The one-page tool arose from a need to simplify all the information that social media folks were shoving in the faces of business owners. For those who aren't into reading the whole book, you can take the e-course, download the document on my website or reach out to me on Twitter. But, since you already have the book in your hand, why not read along and give it a try.

The Social Works One Page System can be found at the back of the book or on my website (thesocialworksco.com). Print it out and have it with you as you work through the book. Each section of the book is set up to help you fill in columns in the document. Once you've made it through the book, you will have filled in all the boxes and have an actionable, easy-to-execute social media strategy document - your plan for improving the ROI of your social media activities.

As you go through the System, you will work through the following sections:

- **Creating a social media plan:** how your business goals and social media goals interrelate.
- **Creating social media content:** how to develop an approach to content.
- **Creating an influencer plan:** how to engage influencers for channel growth.

It sounds sales-y, I know. Yet, after having thousands of students take my classes, I can assure you that nothing makes me more frustrated than the way we have so overwhelmed business owners with bad information about social media. It does not need to be complicated.

Social media is a simple tool that can be highly effective when done correctly. So please, stop wasting time and instead print out the Social Works One Page System and let's get started improving your social media experience, driving sales and winning your business category.

Social media is your playground. You can test, experiment, re-try and re-test. You can delete things (most things!) and try a lot of different angles. This shouldn't be scary. It should be fun - and more than anything, it should be easy.

Creating A Social Media Plan

Setting Social Media Goals and Vision

Why are you setting a social media plan? My guess is that you want to sell something: a product, a service, a message, yourself. If you don't want to sell something, then you should probably get off social media. Every person and brand on every platform is in the business of selling things: their products, their lifestyle, their personal brand. Not only that, but as Lafley and Martin write in their popular book *Playing to Win,* they are there to win. From the book:

"A company must play to win. To play merely to participate is self-defeating. It is the ultimate recipe for mediocrity. Winning is what matters – and it is the ultimate criterion of a successful strategy. Once that aspiration to win is set, the rest of the strategic questions relate directly to finding ways to deliver the win…. A too modest aspiration is far more dangerous than a too-lofty one."[1]

If you have have just been on social media because everyone else is on social media, then you may have experienced the self-defeating mode that arises when you are not playing to win. Instead, to make social media valuable for your company, you need to figure out **exactly** why you are on social media and **exactly** what winning on those channels would look like. For most people, winning means driving people into their sales funnel.

Once you come to terms with that, the reason you are doing social media becomes a lot more obvious. You are using your social platforms to sell to your followers – to attract their mindshare and their business. How you go about that will vary

---

[1] Lafley and Martin. Playing to Win. Harvard Business Review. 2013 (p. 36)

depending on your product, your leadership style and your needs. Ultimately, social media - like TV advertising or any other platform - is in the business of selling things; your job is to figure out the best way to sell what you've got to offer.

This directly competes with many people's visions, my own included, about the ideal use of social media. Wouldn't it be nice if it were really about creating community, driving engagement and starting conversations? It's not.

Rule # 1: Social Media is about sales. This is the first and only rule of social media.

How then do you use social media to drive sales? You create a plan.

Businesses "need strategies and plans of how to execute across social media platforms, in what way and with whom." says Barbara Jones, Founder and CEO of Blissful Media Group, a massive influencer network, "that is the only way they can be successful."

Many brands - because they are understaffed in social, are filled with junior staffers or have been flooded with too much information about social media - don't have strategies or plans. Yet, you need one. A social media plan is a document that you use to determine where you'll be active on social media, what you'll accomplish there, and what your goals are for the future.

Before you can begin to create a plan, though, you need to determine your social media vision and what goals must be met to achieve your vision. First, find out what these are. This should be relatively easy if you are working for a big corporation, as they will likely publish their vision and goals for achieving it at the start of each fiscal year. If you are a smaller company, you may need to sit down with your leadership (or yourself if you're a one-man shop!) and make sure you know where you are going (vision) and how (goals).

The goals and vision of your business should directly translate to the goals and vision of your social media plan. This may sound like common sense to some but it is often surprising to realize that small businesses with two or more owners don't have common understandings of their business.

A few years ago, when I was teaching a class in Nairobi, I was asked to consult on the creation of a social media plan for a start-up incubator hub. The five partners sat with me in a room and explained why they needed a social media plan. When I asked them to step back and tell me what their business plan was, I received five very different - and even conflicting - answers. I explained that until they knew and were aligned on what their business should do, I wouldn't be able to craft a social media plan that achieved results. If I didn't know what the business wanted to do, they would continue to see the listless social media growth that had been the impetuous for the meeting.

Then, last year, I was working with a professional development coach who shared that while her business was growing rapidly, she was struggling to achieve any growth in her social media channels, and she couldn't figure out why. She routinely spent an hour a day on social media and she only saw one or two new followers increase per week. When I asked her why she was on social media, she looked at me like I wasn't listening.

"I have to be on social media," she said.

"Why?" I asked.

"Because everyone is," she said.

"But, why are YOU on it?" I asked.

Then she stopped talking and started really listening to me. Eventually, we determined that she wanted to use social media to build her brand personality so that she could get speaking gigs and eventually publish a book. Now, she has a plan that is tuned to getting her in front of the TED community, interacting with leaders in her sphere and sharing her thoughts online. Her goals of public speaking and book publishing align with her business goals to increase her passive income (i.e. ways she can make money that don't require service) and to enhance her credibility with top-tier corporate leaders.

To be successful, a social media plan needs to have a vision, which dictates a central thematic topic. Customers need to understand why the channel exists and how to relate it. A business vision does this for your social plan.

To determine your business vision, look five-to-ten years in the future and ask yourself, if I were wildly successful, what would my business do? Examples of business vision statements include Microsoft's "to put a PC in every home in the world;" Starbuck's "to inspire and nurture the human spirit – one person, one cup and one neighborhood at a time;" and Tesla's "to create the most compelling car company of the 21st century by driving the world's transition to electric vehicles."

If you are having trouble creating a vision statement, check out Five: Where Will You Be Five Years from Today by Dan Zadra. It's very useful, and simpler than a lot of MBA books on the topic.

I believe that setting a big business vision is the single most important thing you can do for your company. As Lafley and Martin say "A too modest aspiration is far more dangerous than a too-lofty one." A modest vision mostly achieves modest results. And, modest results are boring for your employees, investors and customers. You could be a run-of-the-mill car manufacturer - or you could be Tesla. Which do you think gets people more excited? More interested in being associated with your brand? Tesla wins every time.

When I host classes, I challenge students to expand their business vision using a simple exercise. Try this before you read any further:

- Take a few minutes to write down your vision statement.

- Then ask: how could I expand what this statement accomplishes? Can I make it bigger?
- Then ask yourself again: how do I make that more interesting to me?
- Then ask: would I be happy doing this and if not, what would make me more satisfied?
- Then ask yourself, one more time: how can I expand this?

Having a vision for your business is about having a vision for yourself, for each person who works for you and for every person who will come in contact with your brand. It's also about understanding *WHY* you are doing what you are doing, creating alignment on the why is what directs your social media execution, i.e. the story you tell across those platforms.

Noted author Michael Hyatt's recent book discusses the concept of drift. Drift is what happens when you are living a life without intention and strategic goals. Drift happens when you're floating along taking what comes to you. Drift happens all the time in social media when we do not align with our business visions, and instead waste time tweeting, liking, friending and following rather than strategically acting to ensure the biggest results. Fight the drift by engaging in a big business vision.

Take a moment and write down the vision statement in the Social Works One Page System.

Now, you are ready to create your business goals. If you already know them, skip ahead to the next section. If you don't, find out what they are, or create them.

A business goal is a one to two-year goal that brings your business that much closer to achieving your vision. These are **measurable, actionable** goals. In general, these goals will be focused on the bottom line: they should help you to increase your ability to sell your products and services or fundraise.

There is a business tool for setting goals called S.M.A.R.T. First created by G.T. Doran in the early 1980s, this framework has been widely embraced by the business community. In his book, he says "Ideally speaking, each corporate, department, and section objective should be:

- **S**pecific – target a specific area for improvement.
- **M**easurable – quantify or at least suggest an indicator of progress.
- **A**ssignable – specify who will do it.
- **R**ealistic – state what results can realistically be achieved, given available resources.
- **T**ime-related – specify when the result(s) can be achieved.

Notice that these criteria don't say that all objectives must be quantified on all levels of management… (it) is the combination of the objective and its action plan that is really important. Therefore, serious management should focus on these twins and not just the objective."

Objectives are goals. Examples of business goals can include:

1. Selling X number of products in 2016.
2. Raising X amount of dollars in 2017.

As you think about your business goals, make sure they are achievable in the short term, easy to understand, and measureable. You generally do not want to have more than three goals; one of them should be a sales goal.

If you, your social media team or any other member of your business does not know your goals then they will not be able to effectively implement them. If they don't know how to implement against them, time and energy are being wasted in the drift.

Take a moment and write down your business goals. Now, can any of these be synthesized into just one goal? This happens a lot.

I remember a class I taught a few months ago where one of the students allowed me to use his business goals as an example while I was teaching. On the board, I wrote down all three goals for his soon-to-launch company – high-end diaper bags. His goals were to:

1.) Create a premium diaper brand
2.) Create an audience of people who support the diaper brand
3.) Sell fifty diaper bag this year.

When we broke it down in class we realized that he had only two specific goals. The first goal was to create a premium diaper brand and that involved having an audience or community of people who were loyal supporters of the brand. The second goal was to SELL the diaper bags, and in order to be profitable, he needed to sell more than fifty. His revised goals looked like this:

1.) Create a premium diaper brand that has a growing community of advocates, to drive 100% growth every quarter for the next two years.
2.) Sell 500+ diaper bags within the next fiscal year by targeting celebrities, influencers and pre-natal experts.

The final set of goals were much more actionable and aggressive than the first. They were also clearer and easier for him and his wife to agree upon, and for their employees to take action against.

Think about your goals and refer to the Social Works One-page System. Write down your business goals on that sheet.

With that accomplished, you can begin to create an effective social media vision and its attendant goals. Your social media vision should also be big and bold like the business vision, but the two are not necessarily the same. For your social media vision, you may want to be the *most notable social media page* in a specific field. Or, you may want be the *social media hub for* your specific area. Or you may simply want to be *the most effective digital sales tool* or even *best in class social media practitioners.* Whatever it is, setting a vision helps to create alignment if you are working with more than one teammate; if you are working alone, it gives you something to strive for.

My personal goal is to bring my best every day and I'd argue that to be effective in social media, you need to show up with that mentality too. In a flooded ecosystem like social, the only things that will pop through are the project, profiles, campaigns and companies that are bringing the best. If you aren't playing to win, why are you playing?

Having a vision helps; having goals is imperative.

You can get by without a social media vision; you cannot get by without goals. Your social media goals must directly accrue to the business goals of your company. If your business goal is sales related, as one of them should be, then your social media plan must also have a sales related goal. You must have a way to prove that social drives people to your website or your store and helps transition people into long-term customers.

If your social media plan does not have this as a goal, then you are wasting valuable time doing something that is not fundamentally in the interest of your business. Businesses sell. Non-profits sell. Personal brands sell too. Sales in this case can be a direct financial purchase or the sale of an idea, but your mission in social is to understand how everything you post drives towards the bottom line.

To set social media goals, look at your business goals and then ask yourself *what can social media do to help us achieve this?* Let's go back to the luxury diaper bag example and look at the social media goals as connected to each business goal.

Business goal #1: Create a premium diaper brand that has a growing community of advocates who see growth double on a quarterly basis.

- **Social media goal:** Create a community of over 5,000 advocates within the next year who can position the diaper brand as a premium brand. Use a network of celebrities, influencers and experts to highlight the benefits of the bag.

Business goal #2: Sell 500+ diaper bags within the next fiscal year targeting celebrities, influencers and experts.

- **Social Media Goals**: Use social media to drive 10,000+ interested customers to the sales website within the next year. Explore the use of sales on social media platforms. Grow a network of third-party sellers and referrers.

In this case, the primary social media goals are directly linked to the business goals. Whomever is posting content, growing relationships and managing social advertising can measure her work against actionable progress.

This is essential. Every single thing you post, every image you create, every time you met an influencer or attend an event, it should accrue to your goal. If it doesn't align, it is not the best use of your time - and **time** is the most precious resource on social media.

Take a few minutes to write S.M.A.R.T. social media goals. Here's a simple framework:

1.) What part of your business goal is improved by social media?
2.) How much (i.e. # of visits, # of sales, # of fans) do you think you can realistically grow in the

next year based on where you are now and how much money you will have to spend?

Now put those answers into a sentence. When you have written them down, ask yourself: can any of these goals be combined into one stronger more "uber" goal? For example, if you are a published author and you have a business goal to sell your books, you might create the following social goals:

- Grow a community of 5,000+ fans.
- Grow my presence on social media so that readers know who I am.
- Grow my web presence through influencer reviews of my book.
- Drive people to my Amazon page to increase book sales.

These are all good goals but they could be simplified to this:

- Create an engaged community of 5000+ fans and influencers who can help grow and enhance my online web presence by August.
- Drive XX sales through my Amazon book page by the end of the year.

Go to the Social Works One Page System and write down each goal on the same horizontal line as the business goal that it aligns to. Then review to make sure you understand what you need to achieve to ensure that your social media drives those business goals.

Once your goals and vision have been established, you are able to dive into your plan on a more tactical level, which we will begin to do in the next chapters.

Defining your audience

The next step in creating your social media plan is to understand who your audience is. This is vital because it will help set you in the right direction for determining which platforms you will be active on and where to invest your time and energy.

Consider your business vision and goals. Who do you need to target to make your goals a reality? This will be the person you think of as your customer.

In some cases, that can be a really broad group of people, but unless you are a huge company likely the answer isn't everyone. A few years ago in a class I was teaching, I had a student tell me that her target really was everyone. She ran an organic ice cream business out of her home that she sold in farmer's markets around Seattle. Her hope was to ramp up into a successful online business.

"Everyone loves ice cream," she said. "I think everyone is my target."

"Tell me a little more about the ice cream," I said.

"Well, it's organic with lots of unusual flavors like black licorice caramel."

"How expensive is it?" I asked.

"Around $8.50 for a quart," she replied.

"And what does ice cream cost in the grocery store?"

"Around $4.00 for the same size."

"So, your ice cream is twice as expensive as grocery store ice cream and comes in premium flavors. This is a unique group of purchasers then. It's people who will pay a lot of money for ice cream and these people need to be also interested in the fact that you have unique flavors and organic ingredients. Do you agree?"

She nodded.

"Then, that's a smaller group of upwardly mobile foodies who are interested in organic food. Something everyone might be interested in is zero calorie ice cream that tastes like regular –

find me the ice cream I can eat every day without growing a pant size and we can talk again."

She smiled and said, "Next year's flavors."

I laughed but we all learned a valuable lesson in understanding who our core audience is. When we dove in even a little bit further, we decided that her social media audience would be a sliver of the rest of her audience and instead be focused on parents and foodies aged 30-65 who had a sweet tooth and lived in the Pacific Northwest.

Take a moment and write down who your business audience is. Review it by asking the following questions:

- Is this a specific enough audience that I can target them with paid media advertising (i.e. have you identified age groups, gender and interests)?
- Is this a big enough audience that you can meet your sales goals?

Now, go to the One Page System and fill in your business audience. Note, that there are two spaces there, one for a primary audience and one for a secondary audience. Many companies and businesses have this. The first is the group you think you can effectively target. The second is the group you may target part of the time or who will feel a spill-over effect from the primary group.

Once your business audience is determined, determine a social media audience. For those of you with some social media experience, you know generally who you can and cannot reach online and who has already expressed interest in your product. This is likely a smaller sub-group of your overall audience. If you are completely unsure of who to target on social media because you have a limited understanding of social media platforms, jump to the next section and then return here.

A few years ago, when social media started, it was mostly focused on millennials. Facebook was created, after all, as an online college yearbook. However, now that a huge portion of the world's audience is on social, you can reach virtually any interest group and target demographic.

To determine your social audience, look at your business audience and then ask yourself who of them you can reach through social. (If you need to know more about social media in order to answer this, move on to the next section). Write it down on a piece of paper and then critically revise this by asking yourself:

- Is this audience on social media?
- Is this audience on social media in quantity?
- Is this audience small enough on social media to target effectively?

Take this response and plug it into the One Page System.

Value

You'll notice that beneath the boxes for audience in the business and social media columns are two boxes that both say value. Under the business column the focus is on what value does your business provide to your audience. The box under the social media column is about what value you will provide to your social media audiences. These are two different but connected things.

Value is about understanding what benefit you provide to your audience. What is the thing you are giving to them that no one else is able to? Or that no one else is able to do as well as you? This can be your particular point of view, product, etc.

Think about the example of the fancy farmer's market ice cream. This brand leader provided business value to her customers by exciting their taste buds. Her social media value was more about educating her customers about the wide range of possible flavor combinations, the food scene in the Pacific Northwest and when and where to enjoy her ice cream.

Take a moment and ask yourself:

- What do I provide for my customer that no one else does?
- What is unique about my brand or my brand promise?
- What will I say to people that will provide value to them?

Once you've answered these questions, you should be able to have a good understanding of what your company value is. The one thing you are able to deliver to this audience that no one else can should always be top of mind. For me, with this book and my platform, I give people simple strategic ways to approach social media. I have a strong background in teaching, working and learning that positions me to help people understand social media.

What differentiates me from loads of other social media gurus is the system I've developed which you are learning in this book. The book is the basis of what I share on social media, my blog and various other outlets. My social media value is a direct reflection of my desire to share a simple social media strategy.

If you are struggling, try to complete this sentence:

My company provides value to my customers by _____ (insert verb) that helps them _____ (insert verb). On social media I bring this to life by_____.

Here's how I fill it in: *My company provides value to my customers by sharing a simple system for using social media that helps them save time and money.*

Fill in your sentence, then go to the Social Works One Page System and fill in the value boxes.

Social Media Platforms – the Basics

This section is designed for people who have little or no expertise with social media and need to learn the fundamentals.

There are a whole host of social media platforms. There are the big ones - Facebook - and more niche ones like YikYak or military survivor platforms created by the DoD. You shouldn't be on all of them at once, but rather only on the ones that will allow you to be the most successful you can be for the time you have to spend. As you create your plan, I would encourage you to only think about the big ones for now: Facebook, Twitter, YouTube, Pinterest, Instagram and, if you want to push yourself, Snapchat, LinkedIn and Google+.

Before we get there, it is important to understand social media and who using it at the broadest level. The Pew Research Center publishes a State of the State on social media and is the source for the data below. This study covers 2005-2015 and shows systemic changes in online internet consumption.

Nearly two-thirds of American adults (65%) use social networking sites today, up from 7% when Pew began tracking social media usage in 2005. Additionally, they share the following trends:

- **Age differences: Seniors make strides** – Young adults (ages 18 to 29) are the most likely to use social media – fully 90% do. Still, usage among those 65 and older has more than tripled since 2010 when 11% used social media. Today, 35% of all those 65 and older report using social media, compared with just 2% in 2005.
- **Gender differences: Women and men use social media at similar rates** – Women were more likely than men to use social networking sites for a number of years, although since 2014 these differences have been

modest. Today, 68% of all women use social media, compared with 62% of all men.

- **Socio-economic differences: Those with higher education levels and household income lead the way** – Over the past decade, it has consistently been the case that those in higher-income households were more likely to use social media. More than half (56%) of those living in the lowest-income households now use social media, though growth has leveled off in the past few years. Turning to educational attainment, a similar pattern is observed. Those with at least some college experience have been consistently more likely than those with a high school degree or less to use social media over the past decade. 2013 was the first year that more than half of those with a high school diploma or less used social media.

- **Racial and ethnic similarities:** There are not notable differences by racial or ethnic group: 65% of whites, 65% of Hispanics and 56% of African-Americans use social media today.

- **Community differences: More than half of rural residents now use social media** – Those who live in rural areas are less likely than those in suburban and urban communities to use social media, a pattern consistent over the past decade. Today, 58% of rural residents, 68% of suburban residents, and 64% of urban residents use social media.

More information, can be found on the Pew website, here: http://www.pewinternet.org/2015/10/08/social-networking-usage-2005-2015/

It's important to review this information with an eye towards your audience goals. Are you trying to reach rural Americans? If so, you may have to press harder than those reaching urban residents. The same can be said for trying to reach various ethnic or age groups; if you want to reach niche groups you may have a harder time than if you want to reach young urban residents. However, on the upside, there are fewer brands trying to reach these narrower groups online, so your ability to stand out to them increases slightly.

Each platform has different audiences, benefits and rules for posting. The below breaks down the platforms at a high level.

Facebook

- **Who should use it:** Everyone should be on Facebook, as it has the largest population of users of and serves multiple purposes (especially as a substitute for search engines like Google or Bing).
- **Demographics:** 71% of online American adults; over 56% of internet users; 76% women compared to 66% men.
- **What do you share:** Content that leads with an image. Ask your audience questions and try lesser used tools - like polls, on occasion, to get user data. No limitations on what you should post but know that content with a photo outperforms other content. Facebook video outperforms embedded YouTube video at a rate of 2x.
- **How often do you post:** No more than 5x per week; post at various times of the day to see when your community is the most responsive.
- **What metrics matter:** See chapter on metrics. The most common Facebook metrics are # of likes, # of comments, and average reach. However, your biggest metric should be tracking what sales are driven by.
- **Tips and Tools:**
  - Median number of friends is 155; but people claim only 50 of those are actual friends
  - 93% use Facebook to stay in touch with family and friends
  - Use photos in your post.

- o Become comfortable with the Facebook analytics dashboard – and ask yourself: where is your user base coming from? Are they your target audience? Are they actively engaged?
- o Consider third party sources that help to improve your content like Heyo (contest creation tool) and Post Planner (a tool that mines for content with higher levels of social engagement).

Twitter

- **Who should use it:** Brands with a mix of visual and written content, and the ability to post quickly. Twitter can be an especially useful tool for brands that have news-y content, want to attach to a trend or have a keen interest in customer service. Twitter is the new customer service tool.
- **Demographics:** 23% of the adult internet population and 19% of the entire adult population. Most popular with those under 50 years old who are college educated.
- **What do you share:** Share content that is less than 140 characters. As often as possible include an image. Images on Twitter significantly outperform content without an image. Also, tap into on-going conversations especially around television shows, news items and Twitter chats.
- **How often do you post:** Posting multiple times a day is preferred. However, your content should be relevant to your audience or you risk alienating followers and reducing your base.
- **What metrics matter:** *See chapter on metrics.* The most common Twitter metrics are # of followers, # of comments, # of retweets, etc. However, you should also be measuring traffic from Twitter to your website in order to measure whether you are driving SALES.
- **Tips and Tools:**
    - o Use scheduling tools like Hootsuite or Buffer or SoCu

- o Use Bit.ly to measure click-through on links OR Google Analytics to measure click-through to your website.
- o Use a content creation tool like Canva to create engaging postable content.
- o Find and follow influencers who also reach your audience.
- o Use a tool like Manage Flitter to find relevant users to follow.
- o Don't forget the hashtags! They make your content more discoverable.

Instagram

- **Who should use it:** Brands looking to attract the specific audience demographic listed below. Brands that are highly visual and/or have a visual product. Brands with time to devote to the creation of visual content/storytelling.
- **Demographics:** 26% of internet users/ 21% of the entire adult population; women (29% of online females) are more likely than men to be on Instagram. It's popular with Hispanics, and African Americas and those who live in urban or suburban environments. 28% of users live in urban areas, 26% in suburban and 19% in rural. Of those users, 53% are between 18-28, 25% between 30-49 and 11% between 50-64. Just 6% of users on Instagram are over 65 years old.
- **What do you share:** Photos with limited written content. People will respond to the visual image but have less response to the text box. Images should be beautiful, filtered and curated.
- **How often do you post:** Daily posting is good; brands with relevant content can post multiple times per day but should limit to less than four times per day.

- **What metrics matter:** Refer to the Metrics chapter. Additionally, the most common metrics for this channel are followers, likes, and comments.
- **Tips and Tools:**
  - Use filter Mayfair. It sees the highest ROI in terms of number of likes and follows.
  - Use hashtags liberally and consistently to make your content more shareable.
  - Tools like Followgram can help you to track your stats.

Pinterest

For a long time, social media practitioners have considered Pinterest to be a social media channel. It has all the components – people creating and sharing content, people amassing friends and followers—and yet, no one goes to Pinterest for conversation. As such, Pinterest has become more search engine than social network. Remember this as you develop your plan. Few people want to engage with your brand on Pinterest but they do want to find your content, click through to it and repost it on their boards.

- **Who should use it:** Brands looking to target the below audiences and who have highly visual content to share. Pinterest is the #1 e-commerce referrer, and should be a main platform for those brands selling products to women.
- **Demographics:** 28% of adult internet users and 22% of the entire adult population. Women dominate the site with 42% of online women using Pinterest compared to 13% of men. 34% of adults 18-29 use Pinterest; 28% of adults 30-49 and 27% of adults 50-64. 17% of adults over 65 use Pinterest. There is a relatively equal distribution of users between rural, urban and suburban.
- **What do you share:** Images of products, DIY projects, advice, quotes, and generally, beautiful things curated and shared.
- **How often do you post:** Post as frequently as you feel is relevant. Can be multiple times per day.

- **What metrics matter:** See chapter on Metrics. Additionally, typical measures include the number of followers, the number of likes, number of comments and number of reposts of your image.
- **Tips and Tools:**
  - Pin a lot. The more active you are the bigger results you will see.
  - Create photos that are beautiful and shareable. Its helpful to photograph your product in something seasonally thematic.
  - Create shared boards with other top influencers.
  - Choose strategic keywords to ensure that your content is discoverable.

YouTube

- **Who should use it:** Everyone who has the time, content and money to make compelling videos. Please consider budget carefully as you evaluate YouTube.
- **Demographics:** 81.2% of internet users in the US with 18-24 year olds consuming on average 10 hours of video on the site. Fairly male dominated; men spend 44% more time on the site per month and make up the majority of the viewers in the top 51 YouTube categories. Women are into makeup and skin care; men into sports and gaming. Everyone is into dogs and East Asian music. [2]
- **What do you share:** Videos that do especially well are focused on DIY projects, pets, make-up, sports and online gaming. Branded content has limited success unless its unusually funny or emotional.
- **How often do you post:** The more frequently you post the higher your engagement will be. You'll find the

---

[2] http://digiday.com/platforms/demographics-youtube-5-charts/

biggest success when posting at a specific time every week and letting your audience know about it in your video from the previous week. Get people used to a schedule so they know when they can expect a new video.

- **What metrics matter:** Refer to the metrics chapter. Standard measures for YouTube views include views, subscriptions to channel, comments, etc.
- **Tips and Tools:**
    - YouTube Trends https://www.youtube.com/trendsmap (show's what's top trending on YouTube for everyone and by demographic.)
    - You need to get 300+ views within the first 24 hours for YouTube to recognize it as trending.
    - Use YouTube to help with your website SEO and brand content as Google ranks YouTube videos highly in its search algorithm. One simple trick is to use the CC optional feature to transcribe your video.
    - DIY videos do particularly well i.e. videos that explain how to do something
    - Consider partnering with someone who already has a successful video channel, rather than create your own.

For those of you who feel comfortable in the above or for those of you looking to reach a more niche audience, look at platforms like **Snapchat, LinkedIn, Tumblr, Google + and Kik.**

Snapchat

- **Who should use it:** Snapchat discourages rogue brand accounts. However, you should consider the strategy best suited for your brand and audience.
- **Demographics:** 70% female audience base with 71% under 25 years old. 62% of those users earn over $50,000/ year. [3]

---

[3] http://sproutsocial.com/insights/new-social-media-demographics/

- **What do you share:** Snaps of daily life. These should be authentic, unfiltered and more or less "real."
- **How often do you post:** If you ask Snapchat – never. Snapchat does not want to have brands create branded channels or make branded content. Those brands who have been successful on the channel tend to be incorporated into the Discover function of the channel. For more on successful integration into Snapchat see the chapter on content creation.

  Recommended advice is to post fun, engaging daily stories (remember they disappear after 24 hours!). You can post live from events and share behind-the- scenes info.
- **What metrics matter:** Refer to chapter on metrics. Traditional standards of measurement include total unique views (per story), total story completions, completion rates, screenshots (used as a measure of engagement).
- **Tips and Tools:**
  - When searching for users, do not include spaces in the search
  - The UI can be confusing – ask a friend.
  - Follow those brands like Tacobell; grubhub; saints; girlshbo; easports_snaps, and Cosmo who have seen statistically significant success on Snapchat.

LinkedIn

- **Who should use it:** Business professionals and those brands looking to establish a business presence. LinkedIn can be effective driving B2B sales and raising profiles of thought-leaders.

- **Demographics:** 111M users in the US and over 347M users worldwide. Of those 32% are urban, 29% suburban and 14% rural. Over 50% of users are adult college educated and 44% make over $75,000.
- **What do you share:** Thought-leadership pieces on your industry content that is relevant to your professional or business growth.
- **How often do you post:** Your network wants highly curated and applicable content for employees, workers and B2B.
- **What metrics matter:** Refer to the chapter on Metrics. Popular metrics include # of connections, responses to posts in the form of comments, likes and shares.
- **Tips and Tools:**
  - A must-do for establishing your online business presence
  - A good tool for hiring and recruiting new talent.
  - Post smart, pointed articles by you and your leadership team. Long form content works well here.
  - Ensure you have a built out company page.

Google+

- **Who should use it:** Brands looking to increase their SEO.
- **Demographics:** 16 M fans who are die-hard followers of the platform; 16-34 years old and more male than female.
- **What do you share:** Updates, posts, automatic YouTube cross-posts
- **How often do you post:** As makes sense to your brand; weekly is fine.
- **What metrics matter:** +1, shares, comments
- **Tips and Tools:**
  - Of all the platforms, Google + is the least vibrant except for a small cult-following of people who prefer it to social networks.

- o Few marketing and branding companies have seen success here.
- o Great for conversations with celebrities, authors, and other public personalities who want to do a "Hangout" with a crowd of fans.
- o Google + Communities are a useful tool for driving engagement and traffic to your site.

Kik

- **Who should use it:** Brands with an interest in a 1:1 dialogue with users and in broadcasting to the Gen-Z/ young Millennial user base.
- **Demographics:** 70% male, 20-25 years old[4]
- **What do you share:** Content in the way you would in IM. This is a peer to peer messaging service.
- **How often do you post:** Whenever you are messaged.
- **What metrics matter:** Engagement; number of messages received.
- **Tips and Tools:**
  - o Now you can create ads on Kik in a way that's a lot more effective than Snapchat. The ads are targeted to gender, country and device.
  - o Kik users are willing to engage in messenger and ads with brands; second only to their willingness to do so on Facebook.[5]
  - o Brands who have created chatbots have seen a lot of success on these channels. Chatbots are likely to be the engagement model of the future

---

[4] http://www.vertoanalytics.com/2015/10/the-demographics-of-social-media-properties-looking-beyond-downloads/
[5] https://www.clickz.com/clickz/column/2403229/3-reasons-why-brands-are-flocking-to-chat-app-kik

Tumblr

- **Who should use it:** Brands who want to reach racially diverse urbanites between 13-33.
- **Demographics:** 10% of internet users are on Tumblr, racially diverse urbanites with a mix of male and female users. They are economically middle-class
- **What do you share:** Blog posts. This is a micro-blogging platform on which you either create or re-blog the posts of others
- **How often do you post:** Frequently. Tumblr's users spend on average 16 minutes on Tumblr when logged in.
- **What metrics matter:** Re-blogs, likes, followers.
- **Tips and Tools:**
  - Customize follow and share buttons to make it easier to share
  - Queue your posts
  - Add a view count
  - Allow anyone to respond to your posts by adding a question, so they can answer from the dashboard.
  - Don't exceed 250 posts or reposts each day.

Now, you can begin to determine where you will spend your time and energy. You do not need to be everywhere at once and indeed without a full team of people supporting you and a big budget, you cannot be. You would waste so much time and energy creating the content that you would be unable to do the rest of your job -- you know like selling, creating and perfecting the products that your company is bringing to life.

Social Media Platforms – Where to Commit?

Figuring out what platforms to commit to is often the hardest hurdle for the entrepreneurs who attend my classes. You need to develop a clear plan on a limited number of channels where you can market in the manner that will drive the biggest ROI for your brand.

"Everyone is rushing platforms in a content deluge," says Casey Lewis, CEO and Co-Founder of Clover Letter, a daily email newsletter for teen girls. "It's unsustainable and dumbing down the internet. Intentional thoughtful engagement still has the highest return for customers and brands alike."

A small number of channels with thoughtful content will always produce the strongest results. You don't need a hundred million followers. You do need followers who are customers, who care about your brand and who want to be engaged with you on a daily basis.

In *Playing to Win*, Lafley and Martin discuss the need to determine "where to play." They note that "the playing field you choose is also the place where you will need to find ways to win. Where to play choices occur across a number of domains, notably…:

- Geography
- Product type
- Consumer segment
- Distribution channels
- Vertical stage of production."

You can apply this same thinking to choosing which platforms to engage in and when. You will have constraints on your product and consumer target that will make certain platforms more relevant and easier to win than others. Find those.

Stop stressing and start focusing.

The previous chapter should have left you with a rudimentary idea of where you want to be the most present. If you are still struggling, pick the three platforms where you feel most comfortable already in your personal life; that's where you stand the biggest chance of success. If you watch a lot of YouTube videos already, you will likely have a good idea of what performs well there. If you find yourself drawn to Twitter, you will likely have an inherent understanding of what performs there. Your consumption habits determine your creation success.

When you pick a channel, you are signing up to engage for the long-haul. Anytime you start a channel, you need to commit to it, water it for at least a year and continually measure to see if you are finding success. So, don't choose lightly. However, you can delete an account if it becomes overwhelming or is not giving you the payoff you need for the time you are putting into the it.

Before you commit to any platforms ask yourself a few questions about your social media availability.

- Do you have 5 hours to commit to social media per platform per week?
- How much money do you have to spend on social media?
- How many people do you have who can help you create your social media program?

If you answered any of these questions with zero, you may need to rethink your ability to launch a social media program. You will need at least five hours per platform per week to be successful. You will also need a few hundred dollars per month in the beginning to spend on creating content and growing your channels. You can do it without any funding but chances are that you will see slow growth that may not satisfy your metrics. Finally, you do not need a team of people to create content – I did it all for a year when I had my own social media agency – but it helps to know if you can split that time or if social media will become a full-time part of your work day.

Take the three channels (or more if you are more advanced) and put them into the appropriate section in the Social Works One Page System. See how you are lining this up and that the channels are directly related to your audience (above it) and your goals (beside it). Double check your choice of channels by asking yourself:

- Is my audience on these channels/platforms?

- Can I achieve my goals by being on these platforms?
- Am I the right person to create content for these channels?
- If not, then what do I need to do to be able to create on these channels?

The first two questions will help ascertain if you've chosen the correct channels and the second two will make sure that you've thought about whether or not you can achieve the goals you will create for those channels specifically.

Your next step is to think about how to set up your profiles across the platforms you have chosen.

Social Media: Setting Up Profiles

Setting up your social media profile is about one thing: consistency. This is consistency across your channels in images, written words and naming. Think about it this way: while all your profiles may be different, you are the same. It is like if someone saw you at a party, at church, or at a bowling league, you might look a little bit different but you are still the same person with the same name. This is exactly how it works on social. While your brand might look a little different on Facebook or Instagram or Twitter, you should still feel the same to the user who follows you on multiple channels.

In the above section, you picked a limited number of channels to engage on. Now flesh out the ideas for those platforms by considering your brand name, profile image and the way you will share content.

- **Brand Name**: Your brand name should be consistent across channels and it should be based on your business goals. I once had a dear friend launch a yoga practice. She used her Twitter handle as a part of her marketing approach. Originally, she went with something like yummyyogamummy on Twitter but then when she realized that what she really wanted to do was to do corporate trainings, she had to replace her twitter handle to firstnamelastname. As you go about setting up your channels, create naming consistency aligned to your goals and vision. I think it almost always makes the most sense to use your firstnamelastname or your business name.

- o In the Social Works One Page System fill in the consistent brand name you will be using. Make sure your name is available on all networks.

- **Profile Image**: Your profile image should be clear and consistent. The variant is only the type of filter used. For a personal brand, the image should be of your face and should rarely change. For everyone else, the image is most likely your logo. Again, your profile image should rarely change. It is how people recognize you on any social network. It is often more of a calling card, than your name itself. And please, get a new headshot if you haven't had one in a long time. Nothing makes me eye roll harder than an image that is out of focus, off center or taken ten years ago.

- o In the Social Works One Page System fill in the blank with the profile image you will be using. Ensure this is a hi-res image that is crisp and clear. Bonus points if you can also make it fun, engaging or otherwise provocative of an emotion.

- **Content sharing**: Now that your channels are lined up, start thinking about what you will share on which channels and when. This is as much about the persona you create on each channel as it is about the channel itself.

The second phase of the Social Works system includes a planning calendar (the Social Works(out) System) to guide you in this exercise. Please reference and explore it further, and note here that what you share defines your profile. Consistent and connected posting helps people to understand you and your brand.

Recently, I met a man who sells lawn care. At first blush, this seems like a company not inherently suited to social media. After all, what are you going to say about lawn care for days on end? His approach to content is based on who he is and the profile he has set up – he's funny and he understands viral content. He focuses on holidays like Father's Day or the Fourth of July, and then makes funny ads about them. He'll publish a post of the top outrageous things to get dad, and at the end will include a notice about getting his lawn care out of the way with XX Lawn Care service. Then he will put $20 worth of highly targeted Facebook ads behind this and make $800 to $1000 in sales. His content defines his online brand– he's the funny lawn guy.

In the Social Works One Page System, begin to think about your content strategy but don't fill in anything further until we get to the next step.

Creating Social Media Content

Great content is the center of any social media plan. Content brings in followers and pushes your ideas out from your pages to others. First, it is important to understand why people share social media content.

A study conducted by the New York Times Insight Group established five main reasons for sharing content.

1. **To Bring Valuable and Entertaining Content to Others**: 49% say sharing allows them to inform others of products they care about and potentially change opinions or encourage action. 94% say they carefully consider how the information they share will be useful to the recipients.
2. **To Define Ourselves to Others**: 68% of people share to give others a better sense of who they are and what they care about.
3. **To Grow and Nourish Our Relationships**: 78% share information because it lets them stay connected to people they may not otherwise stay in touch with. 73% share information because it helps them connect with others who have the same interests.
4. **Self-Fulfillment**: 69% of people share information because it allows them to feel more involved in the world.
5. **To Get the Word Out About Causes or Brands**: 84% share because it is a way to support causes or issues that they care about.

The New York Times went on to define key factors to think about when creating your own content:

1. Appeal to consumers' motivation to connect with each other – not just your brand.
2. Trust is the cost of getting entry to sharing i.e. they have to trust you before they'll share your content.

3. Keep it simple… and it will get shared… and it won't get muddled when it does.
4. Appeal to their sense of humor
5. Embrace a sense of urgency
6. Understand that getting your content shared is just the beginning (*Because sales is the goal*)
7. Email marketing is still #1 (*which we will talk about later*)

Great content requires more than just great brand understanding. It also requires a careful examination of what motivates your business's audience.

The 70/30 rule

Creating social media content every day (or even a few days a week) is tiresome! In fact, the average small business owner spends an hour a day creating social media content. An hour! This means that all that time you should spend farming for leads, updating product, or doing the boring old accounting is instead caught up in the creation of social media. This is not the best use of anyone's time.

Luckily we don't have to make great content every single day. In fact, often we can find, borrow or otherwise repurpose great content. "Content isn't king," argues Monica Vila, the social media guru and visionary blogger behind The Online Mom. "Rather *context* is king." Context is about understanding what you are trying to say, rather than just figuring out what you are going to create that day. It's about determining what conversation you are going to have on social media and what conversations are going to spark in response. This is an important framework to put around the conversation you are driving; it will help you determine your **value** to your community. Context isn't just your content. It is about understanding what content from other people you want to surface so you can showcase the entire context of your argument.

To determine your context, Monica encourages businesses of all shapes and sizes to ask:

- What conversation do I want to start on social media?
- What conversation do I want to illicit?
- What or who am I going to listen to?

This is something I have done in building my business. I wanted to start a conversation about how to simplify social media for small businesses. I wanted to take the hardship out of it and get the industry to recognize that we don't make this easy for people but instead inundate them with information. I wanted to help solve the problems of small businesses. Therefore, my channels, the content I create and the apps and tools I develop are all within this context.

To get your head around context being king, you need to understand two more points that might go against anything you've learned in other places. Sharing these, seems like a bit of subterfuge of the current business industry.

1. First, forget what you know about competition. To succeed on social media, you need to make sure that everybody wins.
2. Secondly, to hold a conversation (to create context) you need to become an expert. To become an expert, you need to give away education and knowledge.

Stop thinking about your competition, period. You need to become a partner and involve multiple partners in a contextual dialogue –if you are the only voice, it is not contextual or a dialogue. This isn't winner take all; it's the opposite. To help all people win, you need to become a visionary expert.

You need to give away information. Sharing this knowledge, providing value to a community, makes you an expert. Experts can create conversation. Experts can have dialogue. Experts frame context for the industry. Every one of you are experts about something and you can use this positioning to drive the contextual conversation you want to have on social media. As Monica told me, "You have to act like a leader for people to think you are a leader." This should be the goal of every small business owner out there. Define your context to create your content to position yourself as a leader within your industry.

You don't have to create the contextual conversation alone. Work with partners who are also content creators. I recommend that you follow a 70/30 rule of content creation – seventy percent of the time repurpose things found on other channels, said about you, or directly involved in the context you are framing for your audience. The other thirty percent of the time, build and create things that have real value to your audience and in there, focus on selling your products and services. To track it all, ensure that there is a coordinated hashtag you are using for content created by you or that you've shared.

Using this framework, your first responsibility as a content creator is to do the following:

- **Set up a Google Alerts for your name or your brand**. This will flag when you are mentioned in the news and can help you to find content about you and your brand that you might be able to repurpose.
- **Follow other bloggers and social media channels that align with your brand or your audience.** Regularly read and engage with their content and share what's applicable and aligned to your brand.
- **Follow brands entirely different from yours on blogs and social media channels**. This will keep you interesting and connected to the world outside the echo-chamber (ego –chamber?) of your own industry. Also, it will help you see ways that people are creating and posting content that could inspire you.

- **Download SoCu**. This social media tool (www.thesocialworksco.com) will help to automate the process by finding content created by influencers on various social networks about you that you can repost to your own networks. (Full disclosure: I created this app with my team because I wanted to see this solution for all of you. It is good. Go get it.)

The above will help you with posting seventy percent of the time and this should take less than ten minutes per day. An easy way to reduce the time further is to keep a stock pile of articles, links, etc that you think are useful and then schedule them out in advance across your channels. You can share a single piece of content across multiple channels daily or just use SoCu (← shameless product plug because I believe in it!).

Content Style – Your Online Personality (Tone)

The next stage in becoming a content creator is to understand the style, approach and tone you will employ for the content you are creating on your own.

In the previous chapter, we discuss the 70/30 content rule. What we are focusing on below is the thirty percent of the content you are creating. However, this is also the style for your various social media platforms and dictates what you choose to post as well as what you create. Everything you post should feel connected to your overall brand personality.

There are all sorts of brand personalities that people respond to. Think about the difference in approach that Fox News (argumentative, decidedly opinionated) takes compared to Cosmo (sexy, fun, light-hearted); both of those channels work because they have an audience that responds to that type of tone and style.

For a quick reminder Tone, in written composition, is the attitude of a writer toward a subject or an audience. Tone is generally conveyed through the choice of words or the viewpoint of a writer on a particular subject. Style is the way something is written. It's how you present information.

In the first part of this book, you were asked to identify your audience. This becomes crucial again in determining your content style. Think about your audience for a moment and consider what types of content they respond to best. Millennials are known for their love of quirky humor (adorkable, anyone?). Gen Z is getting a reputation for being smart, tenacious and wanting content delivered to them in smart new ways. Think specifically about your audience. Are you targeting moms, college students or urban female residents who love coffee and puppies?

Think about other brands that resonate with your demographic audience and ask:

- What makes that brand so applicable to this audience?
- How does that brand sound?
- Are they funny, endearing, warm-hearted, angry, mad?
- How does the audience respond to this feeling?

Take a brand like Taco Bell. If I wanted to reach men age 18-24, referencing Taco Bell would be a good place to start. They offer fast, cheap food for busy college students who are often living off a budget. On their social channels, they are fun, funny, and connected to the zeitgeist. Taco Bell feels relevant because they come across as someone's funny cool friend. As a result, their social audience responds back to the Taco Bell handles as if talking with a friend.

Take a moment and ask yourself these same questions.

- What makes my brand applicable to this audience? (What is your value!)
- How does my brand sound?
- Am I funny, endearing, warm-hearted, angry, mad (or any other emotion)?

- How do I want the audience to respond back to the emotional stance my brand is taking on social?

Once you've filled in the above, take a step back and think about who manages your social media channels. It might be you or someone else on your team. Think particularly about the emotion you want to achieve and then think about whether or not you are able to deliver on that emotion. Try as hard as we want, some of us are just not all that funny or angry or endearing. If that's the case, you need to do one of two things – either change your tone so that you are able to achieve the one you want or think about hiring people who naturally have the tone you are trying to achieve.

A few years ago, I spent a few days with folks from GoPro. I was fascinated that they hired professional athletes to maintain their social media channels. These athletes were exactly the consumer Go Pro was trying to reach – but the cooler, idealized version. As a product, GoPro allows its consumers to feel like professional athletes. It allows them to obtain the fame and glory of an athlete, even if they aren't one. So, the brand has staffed their offices with people who know about the time, dedication and hard work necessary to become a serious athlete – only those athletes have done it in a way that is just a bit cooler than the rest of us. As a result, Go Pro has a very active fan community that connects with the brand's social media channels and the people behind those channels.

If you aren't the right person to connect with your audience, consider hiring the right people to do it. But don't just hire an intern to manage your social media strategy. While an intern may understand social media or have the right tone to connect with your brand, she doesn't necessarily understand how to use social media to create and drive sales.

Almost a decade ago, when I first started working in social media, I was one step above an intern. Social media wasn't a trend yet and an advertising agency outside Washington D.C. was looking for someone to do some freelance work running daily social media for a number of D.C. based companies.

"We tried to hire an intern," the owner of the agency said to me as we sat in the hip offices in Northern Virginia. "But no one was really interested. We need someone who knows what to do on Facebook and Twitter and things."

"I know more than some people," I said as I stared at him earnestly and thought of the money I needed to make so I could stop waitressing three days a week on top of my other day job.

"Well I don't even have a Facebook page. We can give you a shot. I would have rather an intern, but I can't find one."

So began my foray into social media. I had to learn everything from the ground up and in retrospect could have used the guiding hand of two successful advertising CEOs to help me get there. At the time, there wasn't anyone else who was an expert and we were all messing around with anything that might work. Bloggers posted about brands for free. Facebook let all posts reach all users. It was a different time.

Now, you can find experts who do know what they are doing. You can find people who are eager and determined. If you do hire an intern, because that's all you can afford or because you believe a young content creator will have the best tone for your audience – train her. This book could be one place to start.

For some people, coming to the right tone and style is a long process that evolves interacting with your audience and changing over time. This is normal. Don't worry. However, it could help to create a word cloud that describes the various tones and emotions you want to hit. Write down a few options from the below word cloud and then create your own word cloud. Pin it up near your computer and reference it as you create your social media content. Does the content you are posting reflect the tone words you have chosen? If it doesn't, refine your post or your chosen tone.

The words I have highlighted in bold in the above word cloud are attitudes that fail on social media. I do not recommend trying to be negative, critical or bitter. While some celebrity and fashion bloggers have made businesses this way, Gen Z and Millennials have little tolerance for brands who embrace the negative. In general, negative brand tones and sentiments work for only short periods of time. If your brand is angry about something and wants to provoke change, you could embrace this tone for a short period of time, drive a cycle and then calm down.

Think of a party: Do you want to hang out with the angry raving dude for the whole night? The one who hates politics, hates his family, hates everyone at the party? No. You might talk to him for a little bit, you might get riled up too but then likely you are walking away, grabbing a beer and pretending you never started talking to him in the first place. You do not want your social media channels to become that guy.

On the Social Works One Page System, write in the brand tone that you will adopt (please no angry party guy tones!).

Content Style – Your Online Personality (Engagement Style)

While your content style directs who you will be online, your engagement style directs how you will bring this to life. Your engagement style is the way you act with your audience. It's the difference between a comedy show, a cop show or a talk show. All of them are tv shows but the style is different – one makes you laugh, one scares you and one makes you think. They do this using funny jokes, dark twisty stories, or provocative speakers (among other things). The content style is your tone and voice; the engagement style is the jokes, the stories, and the speakers.

There are a number of online engagement styles you can adopt and you will probably use a variety of them as you post. However, having a broad understanding of the ways you want to engage will provide direction on a daily basis. In short, it will save you time.

Here are five types of engagement models that you can look to:

- **Prize Machine:** Focused on giveaways, contests and other prize mechanisms. Generally adopted by brands that have limited relevant content, deep pockets and a need to quickly grow their followers.
- **Educator**: Focused on sharing useful information with the audience through articles, teaching tips, tutorials, etc. Generally adopted by brands with deep knowledge in specific fields, and that are sharing their knowledge to drive engagement with their brand or sales of an e-course, books, etc.
- **Customer Service Rep**: Focused on helping customers more than on sharing content or information. Generally adopted by large companies, like airlines with a large number of customer inquiries. When this is adopted by a small brand it can quickly turn fans to evangelists.

- **Sensationalist**: Focused on driving traffic by creating copious sensational, inflammatory or other-wise click bait-y headlines. Generally adopted by content heavy media sources as a means of driving traffic to their websites.
- **Egotist:** Focused on the brand or person who is behind the page. Generally adopted by celebrities, big brands and those with copious amounts of content to share about themselves.

While there are many other engagement models, this is a good place to start as you build your channels – not only who you want to be, but also **how** you want to show up for that audience.

Think about the "**how** you engage" on social media as the same way you would train your employees to engage with your customers if you had a brick-and-mortar store. You would instruct them on what to wear, how to greet customers, how to take care of customers who have problems - and this would all be driven by who you wanted to be in your community and how you wanted your community to respond to you.

These days, your social media pages are your brick-and-mortar stores. Your social media managers are the front line employees who engage with your customer. Spending time to determine how you want for show up to those customers is incredibly important.

Take a moment to write the top few engagement models that are the closest to the one you want to embrace.

Now, write down the four or five words you want people to think about when they think of your brand. This should determine your top principles for how you'll engage online.

Write down the following sentences and fill in the blanks with your responses.

- Our brand will be

  _____

- We will answer questions in a way that is

  _____

- We will lead with

  _____

  quality and want people to think we are

  _____

This is your engagement model mantra and should be what you look at when responding and posting online and what you share with your social media management team.

Now, re-visit the engagement model you chose, make sure it still feels accurate (if it doesn't create your own terminology to describe who you want to be) and then add it into the content strategy box on the Social Works One Page System.

Content Strategy

You may have heard the term content marketing – it's a fancy way of saying "getting your content out there and getting people to read it." There are people whose whole job it is to optimize content and deploy it at the right times and intervals to guarantee that people will read it. Content marketing can be incredibly complicated… but it doesn't have to be.

A content strategy simply means that you have a plan for how you are going to create content, when you are going to create it and why you are going to create it. Otherwise, you will waste a lot of time creating content that doesn't do anything.

There are a lot of great books that tell you how to create content and this isn't one of them. I'd recommend Content Rules: How to Create Killer Blogs, Podcasts, Videos and More as a place to start. They offer plenty of tips that focus on how to tell your story effectively.

If you want a simple tip for how to create great content, take it from my friend Jennifer Braunschweiger, the former Executive Editor of More Magazine. She sums it up by saying "Interesting people make interesting content. Interesting people understand the emotional right now - what the culture is looking for at the moment. The emotional right now is all about understanding the zeitgeist and having the empathy to connect with it. To be good content creators you must consume good content." In short, if you want to know how to become a better content creator, go read really good books or magazines or watch great films or listen to great podcasts.

I post once a month on my favorite books, podcasts etc. because I think it is important to not only read but to continually be in the process of reading something new, sharing the best of the best, and encouraging others to do the same. If books aren't your thing, watch great documentaries, listen to amazing music or go play. Steven Johnson, author of Where Good Ideas Come From, argues that good ideas come from doing things outside your norm. He says in the book, "We can think more creatively if we open our minds to the many connected environments that make creativity possible." In the case of a content creator, you never know where the connected environments might be. So your search to find great content is the search to find connections and comparisons that others might have missed.

Another friend of mine, the behavioral researcher Jon Levy, argues that wonder is the most unique of all human emotions. He defines wonder as simply the connection in someone's mind of two ideas previously thought disconnected. The creative intermingling of those two distanced concepts can produce new neural connections. If you do that, you are creating a hardwired connection in someone's mind – a hardwired connection to your brand. At the end of the day, that is the dream of any content creator: that their content is so good that they can use it to create a deep connection to their brand. This should also be your goal.

But, like I said, teaching you content creation is not the goal of this book. What this book, or more specifically this chapter is about, is how to figure out what kind of content you need, when to post it, where to post it and why.

There are three main areas of content creation you must focus on each week to ensure that you are growing your channel, populating your channel and selling on your channel – and you don't want to do them all at the same frequency. These are ways that you can provide value to your community. To make it simple, I've bucketed your focus areas for content creation into three main categories:

- **Engagement**: Engagement is about creating social media content that people will interact with - meaning they will comment, share, etc. This is the number one thing that people measure when they measure social media posts and so it's often the thing that people create social media posts to do. This is a part of what your posts should do because when people share your content with others, it means that the social media content is valuable to them. You want to create valuable social media content that people do share because it helps you to reach more people and it provides an endorsement for your brand from others. However, this is only part of the story.
- **Sales:** Your content must also sell your product. As such, you must focus at least one day of the week on selling. Share the price of the product, talk about its features vs. the competition, land the value prop and do it across all your channels. This is the essential role of social media for your business. If you do it too often, you'll lose fans. If you don't do it often enough, you're wasting effort. Think back to your business goals – you're on social to sell, so don't waste the opportunity.

- **Community:** Community is the final category of content necessary on your social media channels. You are not an island alone in a sea of non-influencers. You are a person on social media who exists amongst a bunch of other people. You read the same content. You consume each other's tweets, pins and posts. In the same way you make friends in real life to grow your influence, you must also do so on your social media channels. This means that a few days a week, you must shout-out to the social media influencers who are relevant to your brand/audience. And, you must also lift up customers, employees, or others who are doing great things across social. In essence, you need to be a good community member – champion those doing cool things, share success stories and build a strong network. This is the 70% part of the 70/30 content creation theory discussed earlier in this book.

This process of working in the three content area focus buckets shouldn't be complicated nor time consuming. To streamline the process, I've created a second social media tool for you called the Social Works(out) System. Like an exercise plan, this tool focuses on ensuring that you hit your major must-do content creation categories each week. You'll notice this plan has six days of work not five, a sad bi-product of our always on economy. So, you will see of the seven days of the week three are focused on engagement, one is focused on sales, and two are focused on community. This rest day is a day when you should be working on becoming a good content creator. Take the time you would have otherwise spent on social and get better connected to things happening in the world.

	Day 1	Day 2	Day 3	Day 4	Day 5	Day 6	Day 7
Week 1	Social Share	Sales	Engage	Beautiful Things	Emotion	Community	Rest
Week 2	Social Share	Sales	Engage	Beautiful Things	Emotion	Community	Rest
Week 3	Social Share	Sales	Engage	Beautiful Things	Emotion	Community	Rest
Week 4	Rest	Sales	Social Share	Sales	Engage	Community	Rest

You'll notice in the Social Works(out) System, that each day has a headline different than what was discussed above. This is to give you even more direction on what to post on each day. You should follow it in the same way you follow a workout plan that targets legs, back, chest, etc. While it may seem rigid, it is intended to ensure that you are creating targeted content to deliver real results.

- **Social sharing:** On these days, share social media content that another person has created. This is a way to "thank" the community, help evangelize their content and position yourself within the community. Do this so that you will receive reciprocal treatment, which will grow your own following and thus your potential customer base. Plus, it saves you time (70/30 rule!).
- **Sales:** On this day, you sell. Create a clear simple sales message and use it to drive purchase of your products. Even if you have a personal brand, rather than a commercial brand, you are wanting to sell yourself on this day. That might mean a post about your professional skills, a work place win, or anything that

would increase the potential of another to pay you now or in the future.

- **Engage**: On this day, the goal is to engage your audience with content that will stimulate them and encourage a response. Often this can be content about your industry. The more you encourage people to engage with you, the more your content will be shared and your brand will be remembered. You are creating deep neural relationships.
- **Beautiful Things**: Simple. Post something beautiful. There is a constant desire to consume and engage with beautiful things — it's why Instagram exists. In a world of chaos and uncertainty, calm beautiful visuals inspire engagement.
- **Emotion**: On this day, focus on the emotion you want your audience to feel when thinking about your brand. Then create content that elicits that emotion. It doesn't have to be about your product or industry specifically.
- **Community:** Like social sharing, this day focuses on your community. But rather than share someone else's content, you are uplifting your customers, your social community, your employees or other people in the real world connected to your brand. It's a chance to put a human face on your brand and encourage human connections. This content could be a photo of an employee and his back story; a profile of a social media influencer whom you admire; a repost from one of your customers. You do this because human engagement is the basis of community growth; people who feel connected will help you grow – and, channel growth means sales growth.

Print out the Social Works(out) System and place it in your office or download a copy to your computer. Start to fill it out with ideas for posts for each of those days. I've also created a calendar book with ninety days' worth of content posts (find it on the website thesocialworksco.com) and an Instagram channel with daily post suggestions (Instagram.com/SocialWorksCo).

Using these tools, you can create multiple posts at once. I recommend batch creation of posts to reduce the time you spend on creating. Scientists have found that on average, it takes us fifteen minutes to become creative. Therefore, maximizing our content creation in one organized period increases our output and reduces the daily drag needed to come up with a creative concept. To batch create, block out three hours or so on one day and create all your posts for all your channels for a month. Then schedule them using a tool like Hootsuite, Later, etc. You can also use SoCu (thesocialworksco.com) for the days focused on Engagement and Community. In order to remain relevant to the "emotional right now," do not make posts more than one or two months in advance.

This process of batch creating content is called an evergreen strategy. You are not responding to news in the moment but you are keeping a stream of "fresh" content on your social media channels. You may have also heard terms like "always on" to define this approach. It's typically thought of as a consistent strategy that is overlaid by more news-driven creative "campaign" moments.

This book is also not about campaign creation (that's another whole book!) but there are a number of great resources for creating a campaign. As your social media strategy evolves and you become more comfortable on your channels, you will want to consider creating a social media campaign as a way to drive a short period of increased attention to your brand.

One type of micro-campaign is creating "lead generating content" or content that has a call to action for people to sign up for or buy a product. For many, this is the single most effective tool they create for selling online products like e-courses. You create the content once, post it across all channels and then repost over the next few months.

Creating a piece of valuable content once and then sharing it across all your channels - and then continuing to share it - can also be the basis of your evergreen strategy. You don't have to make a new post every day. And you definitely do not need a new topic to post about every day. Instead think about content in buckets. Talk about one topic in a variety of different ways or over the course of many days or months. Some people think about a posting strategy by determining their daily, weekly, monthly, quarterly and bi-yearly content. Bi-yearly they post big reports that are then diced up in chunks for quarterly posting (think white papers), monthly for more topic exploration (think webinars), weekly for minor points (think long blog posts) and daily for smaller points like facts, graphs or photos. In that way, the big pieces of content feed the smaller points. Going back to the topic of context as king – you could determine your contextual argument, determine the big delivery method for your argument and then use that as material for an entire year.

You need three or four months of good content that you can repost across your social channels as you continue to create new content to replace it. This approach ensures that you are hitting all your target areas while reducing the drag of daily content creation.

A few months ago, I was speaking with a student who wanted to make a statement in the field of geo-caching.

"I think we are going to make a big impact on Pi Day," he said.

"Why? What's the connection between Pi Day and geo-caching?" I asked.

"Well, we think there might be audience cross-over."

"Right, but what will you say."

"Well, we really want to share how fun geo-caching can be."

"Okay. What makes it fun? Why would anyone want to talk about that?" I asked. His response was a sort of blank stare and then he shook his head.

"I don't know."

"What if you made a big yearlong geo-caching competition that you launched on Pi Day and it somehow referenced Pi or pies in everything. Perhaps you could partner with the Pi Day people and it would be a whole year of fun cross-over things."

The class then began to spitball further on the topic and he suddenly heard hundreds of ideas for big, medium-sized and little activations he could do online to help spread the idea that Geocaching was a fun activity. From there, he could help his team build out an evergreen strategy for daily posts that mapped to the bigger events and objectives.

Once you have a plan for your evergreen content, you can begin to think about unique ideas that drive even harder towards your goal. Reducing the time you spend on everyday tasks can increase the time you have for exciting projects that will drive bigger impact across your channels. Automate the boring things; create time for the fun things. (I would argue this could be a good life strategy too.)

What might that creative content be? You could make:

- Short video clips
- A series of lead-generating webinars
- Podcasts
- Contests
- Interviews
- Multi-platform marketing campaigns
- A strong influencer engagement campaign.

However, as you are creating this content outside of your evergreen strategy you still want it to adhere to the three big content creation buckets. Anything you create should 1.) engage your audience, 2.) sell your product or 3.) grow your community, and it should fall into the content strategy calendar outlined above. The difference is that you can make more unique, fun or differentiated content when you've eliminated the task of thinking up content every day.

Now, go to The Social Works One Page System and fill in the Content Strategy box. Your first line should be "follow the Social Works(out) system to create evergreen content." Fill in the next few lines with a unique activation you would like to do to make bigger impact than you would get from a daily post: webinars, e-courses, photo campaigns, video. Think about your engagement style and make sure you create content that naturally reflects that style. Also consider your audience and your business goals. While creating a unique photo campaign may be of personal interest to you, ask yourself: Is it the right thing for your business? A photo campaign for a podiatrist might not be as successful as a photo campaign for a local ice cream shop. On the other hand, an ice cream shop might be a horrible business to run a podcast but it could be fascinating to listen to a podiatrist diagnose foot ailments on air.

Ask yourself, if the unique content strategies you listed are really the right ones for your business. If not, rethink what is the most natural alignment, what will have the biggest impact and what will match your tone and style. Not sure? You might have to just give it a try and see what happens – that after all is the best and most exciting part of making content on social media: you can continually try again and refine.

Goals on Social Media Platforms

Once you've determined your content strategy, you need to set appropriate, measurable goals for your channels. While it can seem like a lot of work, measurement is essential to knowing if you are on track, if you are growing and if your content will be successful online.

I measure the progress of all my social media channels every Monday morning when I get into the office. I enter the metrics into a spreadsheet and I track growth over time against my goals. When I'm diligently doing this I see results; when I'm not, I see drops in performance on every platform.

Look at your business goals and your social media goals in order to set your platform goals. Say, you are a no-calorie ice cream brand (first off, if you make this, let me know. I'll be your biggest customer.) that is just entering the market. The below outlines your goal strategy: from business goals to social media goals to social media platform goals.

Business Goals	Social Media Goals	Social Media Platform Goals	Content Creation
Spread awareness for and gain a following for ice cream to sell 10,000 units of ice cream this year	Create 3-5 social media channels to spread awareness of the brand	Be the most recognizable brand for producing ice cream content as measured by biggest share of voice – Over 50% share of voice	Follow the Social Works (out) System
	Create an audience of 5,000 social media enthusiasts in the top three priority markets	Use Facebook to double brand awareness and engagement	Run targeted Facebook ad campaign and create unique Facebook content
	Drive a 10% increase in sales	Create a Pinterest channel that increases	Create photo heavy content and use a tool

		social sales by 25%	like BoardBooster to loop the content.
Create 5 large distribution partnerships			

See how your business goals drive your social media goals which drive your platform specific goals? We only aligned social media goals with one business goal because there is not a useful role for social media in creating large distribution partners. There is a role for social to play in increasing awareness, growing a customer base and selling units. Your social media, business and platform goals are all connected to ensure your business goals are being met. In this case, only one of the business goals was targeted through social media and this is common. Some business goals require tactics and a business approach for which social media is not the answer.

To make this even clearer, let's break it out in the reverse as well. If you run targeted Facebook ads and create unique Facebook content, you can double your brand awareness and engagement on Facebook. This would be measured through your Facebook analytics dashboard. Doing this would help you grow from a small audience size to an audience of over 5000 ice cream enthusiasts against your top priority markets. Having that kind of enthusiast base would meet your business goal to help you spread awareness for and gain a following around your ice cream and drive sales.

On the Social Media One Page System fill in your platform goals as they are aligned to your social media goals, as they are aligned to your business goals. Make sure they are measurable, specific goals that you can track week over week or month over month.

Have you ever tried to lose weight? Have you ever tried to lose weight without first stepping on the scale or taking your measurements? It's basically impossible because you don't have a reference point for where you started and you don't know how to determine success. The principle here is the same: understanding your baseline and tracking your progress will keep you accountable.

Distribution

The next step in your social media content strategy is to think through distribution. Before you start, distributing your content, make sure you have a strong SEO system in place. This ensures that you have well indexed and highly searchable content. For those on Wordpress, I strongly recommend Yoast SEO. It is a pretty standard tool for professional bloggers.

Once that's squared away, here's what you'll need to do:

1. **Batch create content**: create a month of content in a single sitting for publication across your social media channels. Refer to the Social Works(out) System for what to create.

2. **Loop your content**: This is an automated process that takes old content and shares it again across channels. It's a simple way to ensure that old content continues to pull in traffic. I recommend a new service called Edgar for Facebook, LinkedIn, and Twitter. You can also use BoardBooster for Pinterest or Tailwind.

3. **Publicizing**: If you use a blogging system like Wordpress.org, you can install a widget that will automatically publish your blog content to a number of different social media channels like Facebook, Twitter, and Google +.

Automating the task of distributing your blog content will save you tens of hours a month and hundreds of hours a year. You will have more time to focus on acquiring customers, making smart content and building relationships with influencers.

Influencer Strategy

What is an Influencer?

Influencers, generically, are people who have influence over another group of people. There are influencers, online and offline, in a multitude of categories. An influencer could be a social media star, journalist or politician or your mom's best friend. Influencer is now such a common concept that its meaning has been diluted.

For the context of this book, influencers refers to those people who strongly impact a social media audience, big or small. There are multiple types of influencers who can provide value to your brand. These people I will refer to as "Apex Influencers" and "Connector Influencers". Apex influencers are the ones who have the larger amount of social media following. Connector influencers are more complicated to explain and find but I think deliver the biggest ROI.

The most effective influencers today are not the people at the bottom with one follower, nor are they the people at the top with millions of followers. They are people with have moderately sized followings and audiences in more than one circle.

Think about it this way:

- The person at the apex of an influencer pyramid (i.e. the "most important name" or the person with the biggest following on a topic) has a lot of authority but they only talk about one thing, like sneakers. They are your apex influencer.
- The person at the bottom of the influencer pyramid might talk about a lot of things or about a singular thing but they likely have too few followers for it to be worth your time to engage with them.
- The real influencers who provide brand value are those in in the middle who have influence in multiple segments- sneakers and ice cream - and have a moderate to decent number of followers. What constitutes moderate to decent depends wildly on the niche and topic anywhere from

500 to 150,000. Use 500 as the minimum; few people have 500+ friends. These are connectors.

In his book The Tipping Point, Malcolm Gladwell defines connectors as, "a handful of people with a truly extraordinary knack for making friends and acquaintances." Steven Johnson, in his book Where Good Ideas Come From, argues that it is not just that connectors are sharing information across different groups – it is that they are sharing information that comes from a different context. This difference in context – the point of view of someone who is not just an ice cream enthusiast but also a lover of crime dramas and 18th Century Chinese art - helps an idea to spread by permeating new information networks. As ideas or concepts cross groups, they begin to change people's thinking. People's ideas change because they are being hit with information that is new to them. This is the real way that you change broad scale perception, and why you begin an influencer approach.

You need your topic to spread into new audiences. When you identify connectors you can scale your ideas out to audiences where your thoughts, in part because they are new, can make a broader impact. The growth of an idea then comes not from the size of the audience following a specific person but rather from their ability to transmit ideas across multiple channels. Connecting with them allows your ideas to cross-pollinate.

That said, there are times where working with an apex influencer is important. One example might be when you need to generate awareness in a particular niche. Your approach would be to go to the most followed influencer to ensure the broadest distribution to particular enthusiasts of that topic. That will provide awareness, but it will very rarely provide broad perception change, new audience growth or differentiation for your brand. It will target fans and enthusiasts, likely of the vertical you are already in.

Think about the launch of a video game. Generally, you launch a video game telling all the video game influencers about it. You don't go to fashion bloggers and tell them about your video game. As such, you create deep awareness among fans who read video game blogs or listen to video game podcasts or, most likely, spend a lot of time on Twitch. Now, imagine if you got someone who is a fashion blogger and also a video game enthusiast to talk about your video game. That would be a way to hit a new audience and surprise them with something. They are going to pay attention because they've never seen this type of content in their social media streams. That one influencer breaks you out of the video game echo chamber and converts new fans and changes perception. A reader of a fashion blog might think "WOW. This really must be an important game if I'm hearing about it. I should go check it out."

When you are able to accomplish that, you've created a novel way of furthering the reach of your ideas and converting new fans. That is the most impactful strategy for spreading your conversation. Influencer strategy is the strategy of spreading your ideas.

Influencer Marketing Depends on Vetting the Right Influencers

To be successful now, you need to get crisp on your goals says Nicole Smith, who oversees Influencer Relations at Intel and is responsible for determining what makes an influencer relevant for her company. She measures an influencer's relevance, his reach (as relevant to Intel's goals) and his resonance with the audience Intel most clearly wishes to reach.

Determining which influencers to work with is "an art and a science," Nicole says. "You need to have a high level of human analysis (meaning hands on time looking at *who* the influencer is and *how* they operate). And I rigorously vet content so that I know an influencer is a good fit a good fit for my brand." As you begin to determine your own influencer strategy, start with the understanding that an influencer is the person who is the best fit for your brand goals, not necessarily the person with the most followers or most engagement. A great influencer will be excited to work with you, passionate about your product and capable of helping you reach new audiences. To find them, you've got to spend time vetting them.

Crosspollination – Why Influencer and Brand Partnerships Can Help You Grow Quickly

When people talk about social media they tend to focus primarily on the platforms and less often on the ways that they can grow those platforms through building external networks. Instead, they tend to focus on content alone. Content is important but slowly grows community. External networks in the shape of an influencer strategy or brand partnerships can increase the rate of growth substantially. Thinking like a Business Development Manager can help your brand grow.

Business Development focuses on identifying and creating partnerships that can be leveraged for driving revenue, increasing distribution or enhancing a product. If you adopt this partnership based model for your social media platforms, you can begin to quickly grow your community by dipping into the communities of other people.

 See the following chart.

When you first partnering with connector-influencers, you will want to choose one that has some area of overlap. This could be contextual (a shared issue or theme), demographic (a shared audience category like parents or students), geographic. That shared audience represents the people who will naturally understand the partnership and because they are fans of both brands, these community members will help you reach others in the new circle.

Your partner will be your host to their community. The people who overlap both audiences will serve as your validation to the new community members. Then, it is your job to convert the overlapping space to make it as big as possible. The ultimate goal would be for your circle to overlap completely with the circle of influence of your influencer partner. Doing so would mean that you significantly extended your reach without having to find each individual.

Plus, often a well-developed partnership will strengthen areas where you may be weak, in the same way you will strengthen your partners' area of weakness. When this happens, it can add new value to both.

Recently the Vice President of Growth for Biggerpockets.com, Brandon Turner, shared a good example of an influencer partnership brought to him by a fledgling author. The author had two books on the topic of house flipping and was seeing mediocre success. So he reached out to Biggerpockets.com and asked to co-brand the books, re-launch and then drive sales on both their website and Amazon. The result? Increased sales for the author and bigger brand recognition for Brandon and Biggerpockets.com as they were able to reach a wider audience with contextually relevant information. Both sides won. The VP of Growth said that he didn't understand why more authors and influencers don't use an approach like this. He wondered if the reluctance we feel is because we feel we need to do it all on our own.

Recently, I had lunch with Patrick Taylor, the Vice President of Communications at Meredith Corporation. The publishing house that owns Parents, Shape and Better Homes and Gardens. He mentioned how surprising it is to him that more people don't think of cooperative partnerships as a strategy for brand growth:

> *"There are many great ways that brands can leverage each other to grow their connections with consumers and still maintain their unique brand personalities. One example that always comes to mind for me is Oreos. Here is an iconic brand that has been around for a very long time but a few years back they realized that if they wanted to reach contemporary audiences, they had to break beyond their own packaging, and think of themselves in a larger context such as a mix in for ice cream, yogurt, cakes and pies.*
>
> *Whether working with internal partners or external brands, collaboration can help companies not only grow their brand presence but also get a broader range of consumers to think differently about their brands. We've done partnerships over the years with national broadcast companies on everything from consumer polls to events. At the end of the day, these partnerships amplify your message, and they can get you to think differently about your company.*
>
> *Companies need to learn to trust that these collaborations are good for their business, and ultimately, good for the consumer. In an age where resources are scarcer than ever before collaborating is something that companies must be doing. "*

The nature of the internet is such that a person can be a fan of many different brands and likely is, in the way that they she buys clothes at various stores and owns various types of technology. I can like GAP and J. Crew and Brooks Brothers without liking any of them less than the other. This me vs my competition mindset is something you must drop to stay relevant.

Microsoft has recently embraced this new mindset. The company put their products on parity across a wide variety of operating systems. Now you don't need Windows to use Office and particular products are shipped first on iPhone or Android before reaching a Windows Phone. This change stems from a deep understanding that the best way to serve the customer is to be where they are, allowing them to choose what is best for them on the platforms they need. To do this, Microsoft had to go from being very inwardly focused to extremely partner focused to ensure the best experiences for customers across platforms. The result for Microsoft is a huge change in brand opinion and an increase in adoption of popular products.

Cooperative partnerships can be the most effective tool for business growth and an incredibly effective tool for social media growth – more than advertising, more than daily engagement, more than great content. But, it depends on your ability to identify, target and create the right partnerships for your brand whether with other brands as influencers or with individual influencers. Find out how to target like this in a few more sections.

Your Influencer Web: Why Relationship Models Work

Many brands approach influencers with a "spray and pray" model. This means they target a lot of influencers by paying them money and hoping something good will happen. It might work, for a moment. It will not work over time.

Because your goal should be the creation of a web of influencers not an army style, says influencer and social media expert Sarah Conley, you need to think about sustainable influencer relationships. An army of influencers means a mass number of people willingly obeying the commands of whomever is in charge at any given time. They will follow the leader with the money and they will share the messages of that commander. A social web of influencers is a much different thing. By creating one, you are sowing long term seeds that will have a much bigger impact on your brand at a much lower cost.

"Building a web of people is calculated," says Conley. "It's about creating deep relationships and opportunities with a small number of people. Those people will act as your beacons within their specific communities. Then other influencers will come to you. You will be creating a web of people who want to be associated with you."

A web is dependent on the center to exist. A brand becomes the center. The first round of influencers are the first nodes on the web. Those who come next form another node and another circle around the first layer of influencers and the brand. Think of a rock thrown into the water and a ripple that forms. This social spread continues organically until you have a large network of influencers who are in mutually supporting relationships and act as natural extensions of the brand.

"Brands move too fast. They try to do too much at once and we (influencers) can see right through it," Conley added. She says there are brands she doesn't work with because they clearly don't care about her but see her instead as a conduit to her audience. Those are the brands trying to build armies.

"My job is to protect my reader. I have the power to sway people's opinions, but keeping their trust is very important to me." So when brands act in an inauthentic manner, she becomes worried about how that brand will treat her audience. In the end, because she practices authenticity with her readers, she wants to see brands be authentic with her, as well.

Authenticity can be a squishy word. In <u>Content Rules,</u> the authors Ann Handley and CC Chapman define authenticity in the following way: "When we say to be authentic, we mean you should make it clear that your stuff has the stamp of an actual person or actual people and that person or those people have the qualities… that make for a compelling approach to content as a solid foundation for the start of your relationship with your audience. You should also be comfortable being who you are." This is exactly what Sarah means – she wants to work with brands who are comfortable and transparent about being who they are with her and with her readers.

"It's fascinating when you see a brand, and I've been with brands that have done this, work with a big name, big money social media celebrity and yet, they don't get the results they want. Often, it is because that person isn't actually in an authentic relationship with their readers. They don't have real influence because they haven't built real trust." If a brand is searching for a set number of followers, rather than engagement, then the influencer work will be less successful.

As a healthcare communications advisor for the past fifteen years, Steve Campanini, CCO of Splash Media and a former VP at Tenant Health, understands the role that trust plays in the ability of a company to deliver on its mission. Trust is more paramount in healthcare than in virtually any other industry because healthcare is so intimate. In many ways, your healthcare provider knows more intimate details about you than anyone else. Steve believes that trust is built in two ways: transparency in your actions and connection to your community. Anyone trying to build deep relationships with their audience needs both.

Trust and authenticity form a two-way street. Brands must show those qualities and they must look for influencers who possess them. Ultimately embracing an approach that centers around trust and authenticity is the cornerstone of creating your own web. This network will then be your conduit to create partnerships that drive awareness and sales.

Many of you may already be engaging with influencers. Likely, you have fans who are already commenting, tweeting, posting. Possibly, you have people who are active, engaged **AND** have their own valuable following. Have you asked them to post or share content? Have you invited them into your store, sent them samples or asked for their opinions?

If not, get out there and **galvanize your audience**. The first step of influencer strategy is to work with the influencers you already have. If you are thinking about creating a web, it is easiest to start with those who are already brand affiliated. You could create an "advisory board" of influencers who will help you figure out who else to target; they will easily be able to spot the authentic and engaged in their peer circles. As Amanda Duncan, influencer marketing manager at Microsoft says, "look inward. Who has tagged you in their posts? Who has already engaged with your brand by sharing your content? Those people are already influencers working for you. How are you rewarding or engaging with them already? It may be more effective to work with them than to look for someone new."

So take stock. To get started, ask yourself this:

- How do you currently engage with influencers?

- Do you have influencers already who you are not engaging with?
- What would you need to make that a more strategic manner of engagement?
- What would be your goals in engaging more individuals?

Influencer Partnerships: How to Identify Partnership Targets

You might be thinking that partnerships, either with a brand or influencer, sound like a great way to grow your audience and spread information. But it can be tough to get started. The good news is that there is no one way to work with an influencer to build a partnership. To get started, this framework.

1. Do some preliminary research with your community and ask them what brands they have an affinity with. This can be accomplished via free easy tools like a poll on your Facebook page or Twitter account, a SurveyMonkey survey or via slightly costlier social media data tools like Networked Insights and Sysmos.
2. Once you've identified a few individuals that overlap with your audiences – take a look at what you have to offer that person. If you are a large company, money can be a fast and easy motivator towards partnership. If you are smaller, think about what you can provide them. It could be some things as simple as a new audience, introduction to a devoted fan base, your skills as a social marketer or anything else. In short, you are determining what skills and resources you can bring to another business. This is your value to influencers. Right it down in the value column of the Social Works One Page System.

3. Once you've established your value proposition (i.e. the good things you can bring to another brand), you need to reach out. The best way to reach out is through a warm contact. Warning: This is difficult as most people think about only their platforms when thinking about social media. Rather than create community, they are focused on creating more original content about themselves on their channels. This is small-pond thinking. You, as a reader of this book, are moving on to big-pond thinking. Make sure you find the others who are also seeing the oceans, not just the puddles.

4. Hold a discussion with your new internal contact about how cross-promoting on each other's social media channels may help bolster your communities, increase the wealth of interesting content and yes, drive sales.

5. There are a lot of ways to create social media partnerships. They can be as simple as cross-promoting content or as complicated as co-creation of a new product. So scale up or down according to the warmth of the relationship, the interest in community development and your experience. It's often simplest to start small and grow your integration after you've had a few wins under your belt.

6. Set up early what you think a "win" would be. What type of metrics would you be looking for from this relationship and how do you get there? Refer back to the earlier section where we discuss S.M.A.R.T. goals and use those measureable goals to create the partnership. This will help to firmly establish the relationship and to ensure that everyone is looking towards the same end goal.

7. Create. Enact. Measure.

8. Repeat with other new and interesting brands.

To make sure you've got it, use the below checklist in the process of creating a social media partnership:

✓ Research your audience: what brands do they care about?

- ✓ Determine what you have to offer in a partnership deal
- ✓ Develop the warm relationship with a new brand
- ✓ Discuss ideas and concepts for development
- ✓ Set early metrics for success and ensure alignment
- ✓ Create. Enact. Measure.
- ✓ Repeat.

This may look simple on paper, but it is a long process to do this correctly The below chart outlines ways to think about cross-pollination of social media channels, dependent on the type of social media entity you are running and the organization you are involved in. It's not the only answer but it does provide a series of business genre concepts. There are hundreds of other ways to conceive of these integrations and even though you may work in one genre or category of employment, think about various other business types if you want to break your industry models and get noticed.

Business Type	Partnerships	Examples
Non-profit	Often, non-profits can benefit by coalescing with other similar but not competing brands in their shared ideological space. For instance, a health and wellness brand can benefit by partnering with other brands that address their same consumer but do not offer countering messaging.	A geriatric exercise brand could with a geriatric doctor, a geriatric yoga practitioner and a purveyor of geriatric vitamins to increase the types of content and news available on its social feeds.
Commercial	Brands have more money (often), a more	For example, Oreo and Taco Bell

	diverse audience (most of the time) and a wider array of other brands to engage with. So, the focus should be on either a.) finding brands your community already cares about or b.) finding brands that your community doesn't already know but would be interested. The best way to identify them is to understand your community.	have an informal relationship on social media where they occasionally tweet back and forth. Doing so brings out the best in both brands and helps bring to their channels more community members – plus they are having fun. Fun is the cornerstone of great social media engagement.
Individual	Find like individuals who attract a similar audience as the one you are interested in. These individuals may not write, talk or vlog about the exact things you do, but they attract the same type of people you want to come to your website and join your community.	If you are a fashion or beauty blogger, you may find that your audience is also a big fan of wedding blogs, Instagramers who are into #fitspo or who are fans of a certain TV show. Those would be the influencers you would target.

The above chart helps determine what your influencer approach will look like – do you want to create a few partnerships with other brands? Do you want to reach out to individuals in your community to create a network of other individuals who are all attracting your specific audience? Whatever you determine, write it down.

Like all things, your approach here should be directly related back to your goals. Whatever model you look at as you determine your approach will go into the box marked Influencer Approach on the Social Works One Page System. There is nothing specific to write here but consider things like "partner with other X brands who target Y category," "reach out to X number of individual influencers in X category," or "develop a community of X number of influencers to serve on an influencer board."

I used to work with a high-end women's fashion label when I had my own social media agency. They had a very specific audience of wealthy women, aged 50+ and they were looking to get a little bit younger, targeting women who are in their mid-forties.

My advice? Stop focusing on social media channels and instead spend the time cultivating ten high net-worth women with social media presences who could act as their influencer ambassadors. Their influencer approach in the box in the Social Works One Page system would be "to cultivate an influencer ambassador pool of ten top people within the next six months and reduce engagement on social to only repost their content as relevant." This makes their top customers a de-facto celebrity which creates a positive feedback loop.

This suggestion was based on a few things: their business goal is expansion to a new audience to drive high price point sales. Their social media goals are brand expansion and their platform goals are to drive awareness. Ultimately, the best tactic to help them do that (short of growing a mass niche following) is to find the women who already have the niche followings and empower them to be the brand face. They are using these women as connector-influencers to spread awareness.

Business Goal -> Social Media Goals -> Platform Goals -> Influencer Approach

Business Goals	Social Media Goals	Social Media Platform Goals	Influencer Approach
Spread awareness for and gain a following for ice cream to sell 10,000 units of ice cream this year	Create social media channels to spread brand awareness	Be the most recognizable brand for producing ice cream content as measured by the biggest share of voice – over 50% share of voice in ice cream.	
	Create an audience of 5,000 social media enthusiasts in the top three priority markets	Use Facebook to double brand awareness and engagement	Cultivate an influencer ambassador pool of six top influencers within the next six months and reduce engagement on social to repost their content as relevant.
	Drive a 10% increase in sales	Create a Pinterest channel that increase social sales by 25%	Network with top pinners to get your pins included in on high profile boards.

Create 5 large distribution partnerships	

Let's go back to the example of the no calorie ice cream company that we used in the previous chapter. You can see, that I put in an influencer approach column.

Given that the focus on Facebook is to double brand awareness, the influencer approach would want to support this method by increasing connections between the brand and top influencers who have big social media pages and social media groups that are highly relevant to the audience. For example, there is a Facebook group called Ice Cream Lovers with over one hundred thousand users. It would make sense for our no-calorie ice cream brand to find out who runs that group and create a relationship, so that they can publicize their products in that group and attract group followers to their business page. Similarly, on Pinterest, the brand would want to find top notable pinners who run prominent boards and connect with them.

Saying you want to attract 30 top influencers doesn't help you very much. What does is determining what influencers you want to attract, so that they can meet your platform goals and help you achieve your business goals. In this case, the no-calorie ice cream brand would want to attract specific influencers who are influential already about their topic on specific channels. They should be reflective of the demographic audience and show an enthusiasm for ice cream.

If you haven't already, fill in your specific influencer approach into the Social Works One Page System in the box marked Influencer Approach.

Growing an influencer network involves research. You need to be actively part of your community and determining in a very systematic way who you want to engage with, who matters to you and how you are going to approach them. This starts by creating a list of people you want to follow. These should be people that you've identified as relevant to your industry, your audience and yourself. Find people who have an above average audience size and success level – the exact numbers are industry, geographic and interest specific.

For those of you who are thinking about influencers for the first time, you might be wondering how to find above-average influencers. Good question and one that I and my team of developers is trying to solve for you in a simple way. However, until we can launch the right tool, you can manually determine this. Here's an approach I recommend:

1. Determine your industry specific keywords (use Google Keyword). These are likely the same keywords you will use to optimize your blog and web content.
2. Now run a Google or Bing search for those terms. Click to page 2 or 3 of the results. Which blogs and websites come up?
3. Make a list of those blogs and see who appears multiple times as you repeat the search for all of your keywords.
4. Put those names into an Excel spreadsheet and next to their names create columns for their social networks. (Tip: you can save yourself time and do only the social networks that you are interested in. However, if you expand your efforts in the future, it could be beneficial to have all this research now.)

	Facebook Page	Twitter	Instagram	Pinterest	Etc
Fav Influencer					

5. Then, research the number of followers that individual has across the various networks you've identified as

important. Doing this will help you to understand how various blogs/influencers stack up in your social space.

6. Now, filter that list against your influencer approach. Think about the no-calorie ice cream. That imaginary company would want to filter to determine only who is the most influential on Facebook or Pinterest and remove those who may have a large Twitter or Instagram following. You'll do the same against your social media goals.

7. Finally, take those who are the top 5-10 and look at their blog deeply, look at their social media content and ask yourself the following questions:
   a. Does their tone and engagement style connect with me?
   b. Do I want my brand associated with their brand?
   c. Do they seem engaged in a deep authentic and trustworthy way with their audience?

8. Once you've answered these, you'll want to pick five who resonate with you. You should like their tone and engagement style and would want your brand engaged with theirs because they seem to have an authentic engagement with their audience. Add these five into the Social Works One Page System.

9. Now, follow them. Engage with their content and re-post their content (with credit!) across your social media channels. The Social Works(out) System has two days a week that you can fill in with their content.

This approach, while labor intensive, at first will save you lots of time in the long run by ensuring that you are finding high value, audience oriented relevant partners.

When I was at Microsoft, I used this approach to create a small group of bloggers that we routinely engaged with called the Windows Champions. This program had forty bloggers cultivated through a painstaking progress of looking at the entire map of online mom bloggers. Now, there are tools that big companies use to simplify this process. Some tools include products like Trackur, which finds and tracks influencers for you. If you have the money to automate the process, you will save time but you may miss out on some of the learning that comes from doing a broad review of your category.

Growing an Influencer Network: Approach

Now that you are following the community, you should be getting a better sense of who the influencers are, what they are talking about and what they are interested in. A simple approach is to convert the influencers that you've been following into the influencers that you will work with for your brand. You already know a lot about them and can reach out to them with a good understanding of the value that you could bring to a partnership.

However, I have a different approach. I like to have influencers that I follow as mentors and then influencers that I approach as partners. This helps me to have a category of people I learn from and a category of people on whom I test those learnings. Therefore, you are constantly learning and then teaching. For me, this learn-and-teach approach becomes my value-add approach for lower-level influencers and is something I have replicated to grow my relevance and following in many areas, not just social.

Value is the cornerstone of developing a strong influencer approach. Demonstrating value does not come overnight – this, like many things in social media, takes time. In the Social Works System One Page Plan, you have been asked to fill in your value. When you filled it in there, you were doing so from a business perspective. Yet, you can take this and apply it to influencer relationship building as well. You must provide value to the influencer and/or to their community. This can be done as simply as liking and responding to what they are posting or in a more complicated manner like forming a business partnership, content sharing partnership or paying them money (see previous section).

There are different levels benefits of paid vs unpaid models of influencer engagement – because I'm always focused on the most cost effective model, I tend to lean towards free relationships if you can. An unpaid influencer management approach is about finding and providing mutual value. It's difficult to do but helps creates what I believe are the longest lasting and most authentic relationships. Try to provide value in other ways – even if you are just a business starting out you might have product to share, an offline network they can tap into, an event they wouldn't otherwise be invited to or another valuable addition not related to this business like marketing or photography skills. Use those value-add skills to be there for the influencer, well before you ever ask that influencer for a favor.

Determine your value and fill it in on the value square under the influencer strategy column. Only once you've established value add, should you reach out and begin to engage with the influencer. At that time, you can ask them to promote or share your content – and if you have built content for their audience already they may want to share it or have shared it already without you asking. This is when you start to create a value added relationship on both sides and the power of a cross-pollinated network comes to life. Cross-sharing allows each of your audiences to find and discover new things and then they begin to merge and grow. Your influencer will see this; you will see this and your relationship will also grow and blossom. This is the place where you sit back and see channel growth.

That's the rose colored glasses point of view. However, sometimes if doesn't work quite like that.

If it isn't working it is likely due to one or two things. Either you targeted the wrong influencers, the influencer's audience shifted, your audience shifted, your content wasn't applicable or the influencer fan base wasn't interested in another point of view. All of these have happened to me with influencer strategies I have created for various brands. The trick is to go back to the beginning and start again or if your relationship is good enough with the influencer(s) to ask them for advice on who else to engage with.

Only through giving this a shot will you begin to see channel growth and figure out how your influencer strategy needs to evolve. Social media is constantly evolving and the people who were right for your audience one day may not be right for them the next. However, the more authentic effective relationships you have created, the more successful you will be in finding the influencers who have strong audiences. Those are the audiences you will want to tap.

Now, fill in your top five audience targets for your influencer approach in the Social Works One Page System, or go do the research necessary to fill it in.

Growing an Influencer Network: Goals

And, now, for the final time we will talk about goals, I promise! Your influencer strategy needs to have goals. These goals, especially in regards to influencer engagement, need to be specific, timely and measureable – for reference, look back at creating S.M.A.R.T. goals. In this section particularly, setting S.M.A.R.T. goals is important because success in the world of influencer engagement is ill-defined generally.

Does having twenty-five coffee dates with twenty-five influencers help you if no one posts about your brand? Does engaging with two influencers help if they become huge champions of your brand? Does engaging with an influencer matter if it drives no traffic back to your blog?

Let's go back to the ice cream example. We will use that brand to illustrate what you should look to when setting your influencer strategy goals. Refer to the following chart.

Business Goals	Social Media Goals	Social Media Platform Goals	Influencer Goals
Spread awareness for and gain a following for ice cream to sell 10,000 units of ice cream this year.	Create social media channels to spread brand awareness.	Be the most recognizable brand for producing ice cream content as measured by biggest share of voice – over 50% share of voice.	
	Create an audience of 5,000 social media enthusiasts in the top three priority markets	Use Facebook to double brand awareness and engagement	Develop 5 influencer relationships on Facebook, that drive a 2% increase in traffic to the Facebook page and helps increase brand awareness among the influencer's audience.
	Drive a 10% increase in sales	Create a Pinterest channel that increase social sales by 25%	Engage with 5 top Pinners to get content on 5 top audience relevant boards to drive a 5% increase in web traffic.
Create 5 large			

distribution partnerships	

In the above example, the influencer goals set are strategic, actionable and tied to a specific business result that will help to land the business goals. This is not randomly meeting and engaging with people because they have big social media followings. Because influencer relations is a new field, there are a lot of people who are "spraying and praying" as we said. Engaging with influencers in a targeted manner will help you reduce effort and ensure targeted results.

"You have to look at the ROI. You are responsible for that," says Barbara Jones, Founder and CEO of Blissful Media Group, which oversees one of the largest and most influential blogger networks in the country. Setting up your strategy and determining how and why to engage with influencers will ultimately create relationships in which influencers can give you better results. Understanding your goals helps them to help you address them.

Enter your goals in the Social Works One Page System.

Sometimes Paying Influencers Is the Best Approach

In the above model, I argue for a value-driven long term influencer approach that can deliver the biggest success for small businesses. However, there are times when a paid model of influencer engagement works best and there are networks on which a paid relationship is the only relationship.

Logan Paul, the Vine star, social media personality and actor, recently shared that Viners have a strict "no free brand deals" strategy. He will gray out a logo, turn around a t-shirt or remove items that might be considered free branding to uphold the commitment that he and other Viners have to the strategy. As a result, he only does brand deals where he has been paid to include product. He is very strategic about this approach, and only does five to eight brand deals a year.

If Vine is your audience, you are most likely going to have to pay to work with an influencer. This can be a valuable approach because you can control the message and content. But even if you pay, I still encourage you to follow a value-add influencer approach. Have payment be a value-add to an already strong relationship.

One of the ways to find a value-add relationship is to not pay the influencer to endorse you, but to pay an influencer to create or curate something that you cannot. In the case of Vine, video is expensive to create. Brands are spending top dollar already, so when you get a Viner to create a video for you, you save time and money because you are getting content, awareness of what resonates with this audience, and posting to the influencer's channels (often included).

In a recent conversation, Barbara Jones argued that the model of influencer engagement is broken. Right now we have passive relationships with influencers: we ask influencers to post content for our brand, they post and then the relationship is done. But, what if these relationships transitioned from passive to active? What if we worked with influencers to fill a different brand need and become our content creators?

Jones described a model in which brands would put influencers on a small retainer. If you did that, you would have influencers waiting for you when you are ready for them. This gives them time to learn about your brand, understand your content and figure out what you are looking to achieve on social media. Then you would not only come to them with ideas of what you would like to see on social, but you would also engage in a RFP process where they could advise you. "Give these people a job with real deliverables, and treat them as professionals," says Jones. "Make them be your content team. Trust them as superstar content creators who have successfully done this already. Get them on your team."

"Original content by you or for you is – hands down – an organization's BFF," says Kristina Halverson in Content Strategy for the Web. "It's the richest and most valuable content that you can publish…. When you take the time to really understand your audience, create content that's uniquely yours; then deliver your content in formats that engage and motivate; you're delivering the kind of user experience that will bring people back for me." Finding influencers who are natural content creators and leveraging their skills for your brand can help bolster your online success.

This model can be scaled up or down. The most important thing to take into account here is the difference in the way that we currently work with influencers versus the way that we could work with them. Don't just pitch them as you would a magazine outlet but think of them like micro-agency partners or in-house social media teams. Let influencers be your evangelists and your content creators. If you pay them, you build a different style of engagement. Amanda Duncan, Influencer Strategist for Microsoft, notes that there are opportunities for every brand, whether its budget is large or small. It's just a matter of determining the most affordable option with the best results.

This is the theory behind an app that my team and I have launching in August 2016. Influencers are inherently better content creators than many business owners, especially those who do not have a content creation focus to their business. Hiring an influencer to take your brand's photos, help write your brand content and then share those images, is a useful way to reduce the burden on you and support an influence. It is a solution to simplify social media by solving the content creation burden and simplifying the task of finding influencers.

Advertising – An Imperative For Growth

Let's get down to the dirty little secret – advertising! In social media, the prevailing ideology has been that it should be free – if your content is good enough then you will attract followers. That is partially true; it is also partially false. If your content is good enough you **will** attract followers; unfortunately, it will be at a slow rate. There is always the edge case where viral content spells massive growth instantly (Dollar Shave Club or Laughing Chewbacca Mask Lady) but for most brands, it will be an uphill battle to get even a small amount of followers.

In the battle for followers, the most effective weapon is advertising. Let's break it down:

1. Do you need advertising?
This goes back to the business and social media goals, that you were asked to set in part 1. Look at those goals and then ask yourself the questions listed below. Determine if your response would be yes or no.

- Do you hope to see (or need to see) rapid (i.e. 3x or more increase) in followers within the next six months?
- Do you hope to see (or need to see) rapid (i.e. 3x or more increase) in followers within the next six months?
- Do you hope to see (or need to see) rapid (i.e. 3x or more increase) in followers within the next six months?

If you checked yes one time or more times, then consider social advertising as a facet of your plan. It drives growth a lot faster than an unpaid, organic strategy which can take years.

2. What would advertising look like if you were to do it?

Social media advertising can take a number of different forms (side bar ads, boosted posts, in channel posts) and it can serve a number of different purposes. Amongst the different purposes are:

- **Fan Acquisition/Engagement:** Help to grow your followers through advertising that targets a specific demographic and asks them to follow or like.
- **Website Traffic/Conversion:** Help to drive traffic to your website in the same way that any other type of online ad does.
- **Post Reach/Engagement:** Help to boost a particular post by increasing the chances that more people will see it.

Within these three key categories there are a number of more discrete actions you can take. Overall social advertising will help you acquire fans, drive traffic and increase the number of eyeballs on a specific piece of content.

You can run all three types of advertising but if your budget it smaller you may want to only one or two types at a time. If that's the case, then you need to figure out which one of these will have the biggest result. Choosing this is largely dependent on understanding how these results will affect your business.

How do you figure out what's right for you? Let's break the categories down further.

	Fan Acquisition	Website Traffic	Post Reach
Why	Creating a bigger Facebook page can create the illusion (or the reality)	Increasing better Google's understanding of your relevance - which will	Boosting the reach of a specific post helps to get more eyeballs on your content.

	that you have a big and successful customer base. It is also an ongoing community of people who will be receptors of your content - i.e. a captive audience of consumers	increase your visibility in page ranks. More traffic means that search engines believe you have more authority and are more relevant.	This is useful when you are trying to get more people engaged and naturally sharing and consuming your content.
But why for business?	More consumers on your channels means more opportunities to promote your brand, create product evangelists and drive sales.	More web authority means higher ranking in search results which means the potential for more eyeballs and more sales.	More engagement with your content means that there are more people who consumed what you shared. This means that they will have your brand and your message top of mind when it comes to purchasing.

In short?	Best path to long term community growth and hopefully sales.	Most immediate path to raising traffic and sales.	Best path to product and message retention.
Next steps?	Test Facebook ads.	Test Google and Pinterest ads.	Test Facebook, Pinterest or Twitter ads.

3. How much advertising can you squeak by with?

You don't have to spend hundreds of thousands or even thousands of dollars on advertising but, you likely have to spend something when you are starting out and looking to grow your community. The simple truth is that it's hard to stand out online. New pages rarely get the visibility you'd hope for.

My friend, an author of a fiction novel who recently launched her Facebook channel, spends about $20/week on advertising. So far each new fan has cost her about a dollar. Because her book sells for $20, if she can convert each new fan to a purchaser, she will see a significantly higher ROI for the dollar spent. Even if just one out of twenty fans buys her book, she still has a net positive return immediately and the long term benefit of an active fan pool for future books. She is not paying for fans! She is advertising her channel to Facebook users so that they can find her page and choose whether or not to become her Facebook fan. You will likely want to employ a similar strategy. To do so, go into your Facebook page dashboard, click **Ads Manager** on the left. The system will then guide you through the process to get started.

Additionally, I've worked with a number of brands who use Pinterest as an advertising platform. This is an interesting way to boost your website traffic and engagement. Pinterest can be viewed as more of a search engine than a social network, as I discussed earlier. For many brands it is the number one e-commerce driver. If you have consumer products for sale, this is a must test. Great boosted posts on Pinterest (bright, long vertical images) can see massive increases in traffic and conversion. To do this, log into Pinterest. Then click **Ads** on the upper left hand task bar. Their system will walk you through what to do.

The beauty of social media advertising is that you can set up the advertising to align with your specific business goals. Therefore, you can target advertising for growth of your social media channels or traffic to your website. So, play around. You can A/B test your content by trying out different types of ads and seeing the results you get. For a full primer on A/B testing methodology refer to the blog post by KISS Metrics on A/B testing or check out A/B Testing The Most Powerful Way to Turn Clicks into Customers by Dan Siroker.

Fill in your advertising goals into the appropriate box in the Social Works One Page System.

4. How do you create the right type of advertising?

Advertising creation is the whole reason advertising agencies are in business. It's not easy. First, focus on headlines – a poorly crafted headline will immediately turn away over 90% of users. Not to mention, 5 out of 7 people will only read the headline before sharing a post or other advertising boosted content. Secondly, focus on simple images. These images should say something without text. Find a picture that is sharp, clear and evocative.

For more ideas on advertising, I'd suggest reading deeply about David Ogilvy, the father of modern advertising, or following some of the major social networking tools like Hoostuite for their downloadable PDFs and guides on the topic.

Key Performance Indicators – KPIs

The last aspect of the Social Works One Page System are the boxes on the bottom of the chart focused on KPIs. KPI stands for Key Performance Indicator. A KPI is a metric used to determine the success of program within a business or organization. It is the number you use to evaluate whether or not you have reached your goals, and will be reflective of how far or near you are to achieving your business vision.

Many of your KPIs will be directly reflected in what you previously wrote for your business goals, advertising and social media goals. KPIs are the top line-aspects of your business that you are using to measure all of the work you have been doing; they indicate if you are effective or not. This is a critical step that many businesses ignore. That's why social media is often misunderstood, not properly measured and can deliver less than optimal ROI.

Now that you've gone through the whole process, scribbled out things that didn't work and updated your ideas, write in how you will measure success. Which KPIs you will use? While I've been using an example with a specific consumable good, this also applies to personal branding. In that case, you are selling yourself and while you may not be able to directly measure results, you can measure impact. Impact in this form could be: the size of your network increasing, new opportunities for jobs or invitations to various other events. In short, there is a way to measure everything but you must decide what the important items are to measure. To illustrate a simple example, let's go back to the ice cream.

As a reminder, we've established goals across each strategic area necessary for the creation of the plan: Business Goals, Social Media Goals, Platform Goals and Influencer Goals. We decided to pursue only one of our business goals through social media and thus all social, platform and influencer goals are tied to that.

	Business	Social Media	Social Media Platform	Influencer
Goals	Spread awareness for and gain a following for ice cream to sell 10,000 units of ice cream this year.	Create 3-5 social media channels to spread awareness of the brand.	Be the most recognizable brand for producing ice cream content as measured by biggest share of voice – Over 50% share of voice	
		Create an audience of 5,000 social media enthusiasts in the top three priority markets	Use Facebook to double brand awareness and engagement	Develop 5 influencer relationships on Facebook, that drive a 2% increase in traffic to the Facebook page and help increase brand awareness among the influencer's audience.

		Drive a 10% increase in sales	Create a Pinterest channel that increases social sales by 25%	Engage with 5 top Pinners to get content on 5 top audience relevant boards to drive a 5% increase in web traffic.
KPIs	Awareness as measured by XX tool Number of online followers Number of email subscribers	Social Media engagement Number of online followers in priority markets Number of Sales	Awareness as measured by XX tool Awareness as measured by XX tool Sales as measured through XXX tool	# of influencer relationships % Growth in traffic attributable to influencers

The KPIs are then taken directly from our planning document to help us establish that we are reaching those goals. Remember in math class when you would have to check the answer by doing the problem backwards? This is the same thing. It's using the result to verify that you met the goals and ensuring that your goals are helping you achieve financial success. They shouldn't be scary – they should be exciting. Using your KPIs to measure and hit your goals means that you are succeeding, that your social platform is growing and that your business is taking off --- congratulations! Go you!

Conclusion: The Practical In Place – What Do You Do Now

Phew! You made it through the practical part of this book. You've learned to adopt the Social Works One Page System, to create a social media strategy that is tied to your business goals and can deliver results that will help your business to be successful. Here are the top five takeaways that I hope you leave with:

- **Simplicity**: Simplify the social media world by making a strategic plan that can guide you or whomever you hire to manage your social media channels.
- **Set Goals**: Set S.M.A.R.T. goals and targets across your social media channels to ensure that social media is effectively helping you to meet your business goals.
- **Measure**: Measure frequently to test the effectiveness of your channels.
- **Influencers**: Work with influencers, engage with them, and grow an influencer community. Don't underestimate the power of your influencer web as a tool for increasing the effectiveness of your social media channels. Your influencer strategy is your news distribution strategy. Your influencer strategy can also be your content creation strategy.
- **Play Around**: Social Media is supposed to be fun! It's there to test, play with and to keep iterating on the posts, the content, the tone, and the images as you learn more and receive more responses from your growing community. Make

room for the creative part of this process by automating as many things as possible through batching, looping, and scheduling.

Now, that you've simplified the world of social media and learned exactly what to do to create big results, what's next?

- Dive deeper into the topic with my Social Media for Sales E-Course
- Join my mailing list
- Join my social media communities
- Ask me questions directly on Twitter

All of that you can find through the website at thesocialworksco.com. And, pay attention for additional books to come over soon, including one on how to make money with your side hustle and another about how to become a successful influencer.

Tools

The Social Works One Page System

Business vision:	Social Media Vision:	Platforms 1. 2. 3.	Influencer Approach:
Business Goals: 1. 2. 3.	Social Media Goals: 1. 2. 3.	Brand Name: Profile Image: Bio: Brand tone:	Influencers you follow: 1. 2. 3. 4.
Business Audience: Primary: Secondary:	Social Media Audience: Primary: Secondary:	Your content style:	Influencers/Networks: 1. 2. 3. 4. 5.

Value Add:	Value Add:	Content Strategy 1. 2. 3.	Influencer Goals: 1. 2. 3. 4. 5.
KPIS of Business Goals:	KPIS of Social Media:	Goal on each platform: 1. 2. 3.	Value Add:
			KPIs of Cross-pollination strategy:

The Social Works(Out) System

Please refer to TheSocialWorksCo.com to download a h-res version of the Social Works(Out) System.

Commonly Used Jargon Terms That You May Want Defined

- Channel: Your Facebook page, Twitter profile or other. It's a specific aspect of a social media platform that you own.
- Chatbot: A computer program designed to simulate conversation with human users, especially over the Internet.

- Content Marketing: Using content to increase web traffic for a brand.
- Key Performance Indicator (KPI): A metric used to determine the success of program within a business.
- Lead-Generating Content: Content that will generate a "lead" for you: email sign-up, download, purchase.
- Platform: Any of the social media companies like Facebook, Twitter, Kik, Instagram. jargon used by industry insiders to broadly describe all the social media websites.

33617033R00060

Made in the USA
Middletown, DE
20 July 2016